MW01608937

THE GOOD APPLE GUIDE TO CREATIVE DRAMA

by

Kathy U. Foley

Mara Lud

Carol Power

illustrated by **Kathy U. Foley**

Cover by Nancee Volpe

ISBN No. 0-86653-030-4

GOOD APPLE
A Division of Frank Schaffer Publications, Inc.
23740 Hawthorne Boulevard
Torrance, CA 90505

TO CREATIVITY · · · · · · · ·

YOURS AND OURS

TABLE OF CONTENTS

CREATIVE DRAMA···WHO ME ?

Creative Drama ----- Sure, I've heard a lot about it. Sounds like a great classroom activity --- provides concrete language experiences, motivates learners, promotes independent thinking. Creative drama in my classroom? I'd like to try it BUT.....I wouldn't know where to begin, it takes too much time, I wouldn't know how to get started, I'm not really creative. Besides, I have 28 energetic students crammed into one very crowded classroom. And most of all, I'M NOT THE RIGHT "TYPE"!

Sound familiar? These were our words not long ago. You ARE the type. It's for EVERYONE. The instructions and lessons provided in this book will enable you to integrate creative drama into your curriculum immediately.

Enjoy,

Mara Lyd

Carol Power

Kathy Foley

INTRODUCTION

WHAT IS CREATIVE DRAMA?

Creative drama is informal, spontaneous, enactments of stories, poems, ideas, real events and anything else that interests you. It is creative interactions among students which include expressions and movements that the students plan and carry out while the teacher suggests activities and acts as a guide. In creative drama, it is the *enacting* rather than the *enactment* that is the important element.

WHY SHOULD I USE CREATIVE DRAMA?

Creative drama promotes the growth and development of the students in an enjoyable way. It provides students with concrete listening, learning, and speaking experiences, further develops communication skills, increases confidence which builds an improved self-image, promotes greater comprehension and retention, and is easily integrated into an already existing curriculum.

WHERE DOES IT FIT INTO MY CURRICULUM?

Today's curriculums are already crowded. We are not suggesting another addition to yours. Creative drama can be a part of your existing curriculum, a part of almost any subject area. It's a strategy/technique to be used to introduce, develop, or culminate lessons/units as you teach. Creative drama will broaden many lessons and add enjoyment for you and the students.

I DON'T KNOW WHERE TO START.

You're already doing it! Do you ever use finger plays, puppets, or have the students make masks? In literature do you ever have the students make sound effects or echo story lines while you read the story out loud? In their reading, do you encourage them to use voice inflection to create the character's feelings and reflect the mood of the story? If you have answered "Yes" to any of these questions, then you already have the beginnings of early creative drama work.

Start small - it can grow and be shaped at your own rate and fitted into your individual classroom needs. To gain greater comfortability for both you and the students, we suggest you start with short, pre-drama activities. These are Mirroring, Self-space, Transitions, Oh-up, Oh-down, and Trying On Characters (see pages 8, 12, 14, 18, 20).

MY CLASSROOM'S TOO CROWDED!

Hallways and gymnasiums are not necessary for creative drama. Utilize the space you have. Your classroom is sufficient. Many pre-drama activities can be done with the students either seated or grouped on the floor near the teacher - for example, imitation of character voices, hand or arm gestures and facial expressions. The aisles and peripheral areas can be used for other activities such as self-space, transitions and role playing. When an open space is needed for group pantomimes or story dramatization, it may be necessary to move a minimal amount of furniture. Often furniture can become boundaries or part of the scenery.

SOUNDS LIKE A LOT OF MOVEMENT TO ME! CAN I HANDLE IT?

Creative drama can easily be implemented into your style of teaching. As in all other activites, a standard of behavior should be set. A good starting point in establishing creative drama control would be to develop a set of signals for you and your classroom. For example, use Freeze, Unfreeze or turn off the lights whenever you need their attention in order to give directions. The cues should be used to give both positive and negative feedback. Once you have established your management cues and have taught the lesson on Self-space found in this book on page 12, desired movement about the room will be easily maintained.

HOW OFTEN SHOULD I USE CREATIVE DRAMA?

Creative drama should be used often enough to make it a regular classroom event rather than the "big deal" it will be the first few times you use it. Because it's a part of any subject area as well as a transition activity, there isn't a special time set aside for just creative drama. As creative drama is integrated with the already existing content areas, it will achieve the "norm" status. Through this added dimension comprehension, retention and enjoyment will be increased.

Some days a particular lesson can seem to be floundering for you or your students. When this happens it is quite permissible to defer the drama portion of the lesson until a later time or not at all if you have passed that point in your instructional scheme. However, remember creative drama is extremely effective as a culminating activity and is equally effective as a review technique; therefore the opportunity to make use of creative drama will soon present itself again.

This book is designed to provide you with a variety of opportunities in which creative drama can be used. These lessons require a minimal amount of your planning time. They are presented in a step-by-step format followed by additional suggested activities. Some of the lessons might best be done over two or three days -- adapt times to meet your daily schedules. The more you use creative drama the more comfortable you will be with it and the easier it will be for you to integrate it into the content areas yourself.

Other opportunities to make use of creative drama as a teaching strategy/technique will start occurring to you as you do your regular unit/lesson planning. Use creative drama frequently -- whenever and wherever it does the job effectively. The gains make it a must for you and your students!

DEFINITIONS

CURTAIN UP OR ACTION -   A cue for the students to begin a scene, situation, or action.

CURTAIN DOWN OR CUT -   A cue for students to conclude a scene, situation, or action.

FREEZE -   A cue for students to stop all action and maintain their present pose while additional direction, instruction or positive/negative feedback is given.

NARRATOR -   A teacher or student who relates the sequence of events as they are to be dramatized.

MIRRORING -   One person becomes the mirrored reflection of another using body movements at a pace that allows the leader to be followed.

OH-UP, OH-DOWN -   A structured technique that allows the teacher to guide the students through a series of situations that can be either related or disjointed.

PANTOMIME (MIME) -   Acting out situations without verbalizing. A narration may accompany it.

PANTOMIME WALK/CHAIN -   Pantomiming out a sequential chain of events while moving about the room or within a stationary self-space.

ROLE PLAYING -   Becoming a designated character and acting out a particular situation.

SELF-SPACE -   A defined area within which a child may stretch, reach or move about without coming into contact with anyone or anything.

SETTING THE SCENES -   Defining areas in the room where events will occur.

SIDE COACHING -   Suggestions given to students to help them develop the character/situation they are portraying.

TRANSITION -   A creative technique for moving students from one place to another or for filling a short period of time.

TRYING ON CHARACTERS -   Students become another person, animal or object. They define and develop the movements, feelings and expressions of the character or object they're portraying.

WARM-UP -   Short movement or task-oriented activities to get the students motivated.

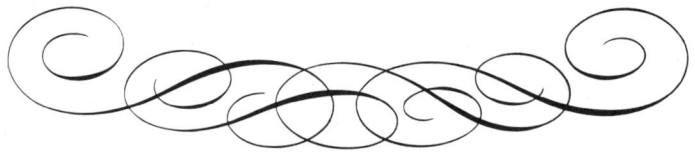

6

PRE-DRAMA
ACTIVITIES

These are activities used to prepare the students for further creative work. They can be used alone as short, one-shot lessons, or they can introduce longer lessons by providing warm-up and skill practice.

MIRRORING

Mirroring is a technique that is just what it sounds like - one person becoming the mirrored reflection of another person. Mirroring involves precise exaggerated body movements at a pace that allows the leader to be followed. It can be used as a pre-drama exercise, warm-up, transition or for enjoyment. Once you have taught this concept and have gone through the suggested procedures, you may use any of the steps of mirroring at any time to either fill a short or long time period. These activities can be done at the students' seats about the room, in the gym or even outside. Once the students have found a space of their own, movement about the room is minimal and since mirroring is pantomime it should be soundless. A-A-H SILENCE!

Following you will find a brief explanation and ideas for mirroring. GOOD LUCK!

A good way to get the children thinking in terms of following a leader's body action is to try using one or two of the following games.

Have children do calisthenics, following a leader without using any verbal directions.

Have children form a circle, one child leaves the room. From the circle choose a leader who will do various repeated body movements which the others will follow - for example, clapping hands 3 times, tapping shoulders 5 times, hopping on one foot 4 times, etc. After the class is able to follow the leader ask the child in the hall to return, stand in the middle of the circle, and through observation try to guess who the leader is. Continue the game for however long you wish.

Using popular music and dance motions/steps, have children follow a leader.

Simon Says.

Traditional game of Follow the Leader.

Before the students can mirror there needs to be a discussion. The discussion should include:

While looking in a mirror, what do you see?

If you move your head to the left, in which direction does your head move in the mirror?

Repeat question 2 except change the direction to the right and then up and down.

What about other body movements? What happens? (Discuss one at a time.)

BEGIN with whole group mirroring the teacher.

Use slow large movements first - for example, hand moving slowly in large circles, up and down, side to side; leg moving up, down, in a circle, side to side move both hand and leg simultaneously. (Young children might want to use the same hand as the leader - right hand for right hand. They will need a reminder or further explanation of what mirroring is.)

NEXT when you feel the children are understanding the concept and are working with ease, then divide into pairs and have them decide who the leader is. In a set amount of time let the children experiment with mirroring each other.

THEN give them 3 or 4 step directions to mirror.

pick up a comb	put a letter in an envelope
comb your hair	lick it shut
put the comb down	put a stamp on it

choose a record	get a shirt
put it on the stereo	put it on
turn it on	button it up
dance	tuck it in
	tell yourself you look great!
	(pantomime)

TRY giving similar situations but make the directions progressively more detailed. Every detail is important.

Open the bathroom cabinet...take out toothpaste...unscrew the top... pick up your brush...squeeze the toothpaste onto the toothbrush... put the cap on the toothpaste...open the cabinet with one hand...put the toothpaste away with the other...close the cabinet...turn the water on...start to brush your teeth...brush...spit...put water on brush...brush...spit...rinse, etc...turn water off... put brush away...look at your teeth in the mirror...pick up a washcloth...clean toothpaste off of face...lay washcloth down...check your face in the mirror again...smile at yourself, you look great!

Open the refrigerator...take out the milk...open milk container...get a glass from the cupboard...pour milk into glass...close milk container... open refrigerator...put milk away, get the butter...close refrigerator, put butter on counter...pick up glass, take a swallow of milk...set glass down...uncover toaster...open bread bag...take out 2 slices of bread, put bread in toaster...push down toaster button...close up bread bag...take another swallow of milk while waiting for toast...pick up knife in one hand, toast in the other...put butter on knife...spread it on the toast...put knife down...take a bite of toast, chew, take a swallow of milk, etc...butter other piece of toast...eat with milk until done...rinse glass in sink...take dishcloth and wash counter top...put cloth down, put knife in sink...hope you enjoyed your snack!

Give students time to mirror their own situations.

———— ❖ ————

VARIATIONS of mirroring:

Have small groups of students display identical body posture or motions - for example, legs crossed, hands on their heads.

AND/OR

As they are dismissed they must copy an agreed-upon movement until they are out of the room.

SELF—SPACE

Self-space is a defined area that adds automatic order to creative drama. It is your safety valve. It will help you become comfortable with creative drama. This is an area within which a child may stretch, reach or move about without coming into contact with anyone or anything. The space may be stationary - for example, next to his desk or in the open area of your classroom or it can be carried around with him as he moves about the room. It becomes each child's private domain, his own castle that no one may invade under penalty of law!

Using a self-space relieves the teacher from added worries such as pushing, shoving and running into furniture, making it safe for whole class movement. If at any time you need to stop the action/movement, the use of the word "freeze" works well.

Once the students understand the concept of self-space it is then the space they will use to try on characters, role play, and do a pantomime walk/chain. Following is a short lesson that will plant the idea of self-space firmly in the students' minds. THREE CHEERS FOR CROWD CONTROL!

Direct the students to find a space in the room where they can stretch and reach without touching anyone or anything else. Pretend to give each student a piece of his favorite bubble gum. Have him put it in his mouth and chew until it's softened up enough to blow some bubbles. Have him blow a couple of practice bubbles. Then you might say, "Blow a very large bubble...carefully remove the bubble gum from your mouth so the bubble doesn't burst...stick the opening together so no air can escape...stick it securely on the floor...Now, close your eyes and imagine you are inside your bubble...open your eyes and survey the inside of it...it looks like it could use a little work...to give yourself some extra room, very carefully push out the side as far as you can reach without breaking it...reach high, low, front, back and all around...make it smooth...now, staying inside your bubble make yourself as small as you can...use as much space as you can...lean and reach in all directions using your arms and legs...Oh my gosh, here comes a gust of wind...it's picking you slowly up and moving you about the room...be careful to steer out of the way of anyone else's bubble...you don't want to burst!...if you do you'll have to find your desk and become the silent audience...take a look at what's around you...look there's _____...wave to him...the wind's settling down and it's gently letting you come to rest on the floor...now, crawl outside your bubble...let the air out...walk back to your desk and find a nice safe place to keep it."

Discussion Questions:

What color was your self-space?
How big was it?
Was everyone's the same size and shape? Why not?
What is your self-space able to do?
What can you do in your space?
What can't you do?
What are the consequences if you move out of it?
(Perhaps as a class you can decide what will happen.)

TRANSITIONS

Transitions can make an otherwise routine task "spicy and fun." A transition is a creative technique to fill a short time period or for moving students from one place to another - for example, down the hall, lining up, changing classes or subjects, going outside for recess or dismissal. These can be done at their own desks, in a self-space, or as they move about the room or hallways.

Transitions are also a good beginning point for both you and the students to "loosen up" and begin to feel good about creative drama. They're short, one-shot, uninvolved activities that can take anywhere from 1 to 5 minutes. In each of these situations "creativity" is your watchword. Perfection is not the goal.

Following you will find a list of ideas beginning with the easy and becoming progressively more difficult. The kids are fun to watch. ENJOY!

SHOW ARM OR HAND MOVEMENT OF A -

hitchhiker   hula dancer

person hailing a cab   choir director

traffic cop   drummer

guitar player   trombone player

disco dancer   tightrope walker

The above movements can all be done while sitting at their desks.

──────────── ■ ────────────

SHOW WALKING ON -

eggs   cotton   nails   clouds   thin ice

SHOW WALKING THROUGH -

mud   water   snowdrift   fine sand

──────────── ■ ────────────

MOVE AS A/AN

robot   big game hunter

old man/woman   soldier

ballet dancer   motorcyclist

ice skater   drum major

baseball player   boxer

basketball player   football player

15

BECOME A / AN

elephant with his trunk swaying

lion stalking his prey

donkey pulling a load

penguin moving across the ice

cockroach scurrying across the floor

snake slithering through the grass

bird soaring across the sky

crab crawling to safety

eel slipping through the water

waiter with a loaded tray

bellboy carrying bags to a room

policeman swinging a nightstick

young child on hot pavement

conductor using his baton

fireman putting out a fire

nurse giving a shot

FTD delivering flowers

grocer bagging groceries

mechanic changing a tire

longshoreman unloading a truck

canoeist paddling down the river

fisherman casting his line

person delivering a pizza

MOVE AS IF YOU'RE MOVING THROUGH A -

bowlful of marbles

roomful of feathers

kettle of chocolate pudding

houseful of bats

can of worms

swampful of mosquitos

swimming pool of ice water

bowlful of lime Jell-O

boxful of chewed bubble gum

roomful of whipped cream

spaceship on the moon

shipload of broken eggs

dumpster of garbage

truckload of styrofoam pieces

You may want to try sound effects with the above.

———————— ■ ————————

MOVE TO A GIVEN TEMPO/RHYTHM

snapping fingers

clapping hands

clicking tongues

flapping arms

a foot beat

nodding heads

bending bodies

OH-UP,
OH-DOWN

Oh-up, Oh-down is a structured technique that allows the teacher to easily guide the students through a series of situations that can either be related or disjointed. Oh-up, Oh-down can be used to role play, try on characters, do more than one transition. It is used so the students can change character, mood or action. This is done by using the signal words Oh-up, Oh-down. On the signal of Oh-up, all of the students will stop all action and raise their arms into the air. It is then followed by an immediate Oh-down. This position is maintained while the teacher gives instruction as to what they will come up as/doing. This will become clearer for you through the example that follows.

O - o - oh-up, O - o - oh-down, come up as a teacher excited about creative drama!

Oh-up, Oh-down. Come up as a postal worker sorting mail...pick up a pile of letters and begin to sort them...oops! you put that letter in the wrong pile...Change it...Boy, I'm glad that's done...pick up the piles, stack them... carry them to the next table...Oh-up, Oh-down. Come up as a secretary typing...you're getting tired...take a break...go and make a cup of coffee... bring it back to your desk...begin to type again...stop and take a sip of coffee... pick up your files...go to the filing cabinet...file them away...Oh-up, Oh-down. Come up as a doctor examining a patient who has cut his leg...What a mess!... Get a sponge, put some soap on it and clean it up...It's going to need some stitches...get out the needle and nylon thread...begin to sew...Oh-up Oh-down. Come up as a lost child looking for his chair in a theatre...Is that it?...No, find your special place...There it is because that sweater belongs to you...Oh-up, Oh-down. Come up as yourself politely waiting in your seat for your teacher.

HINTS -

When saying the Oh-up, Oh-down let your voice raise up slowly on Oh-up, pause, and then slowly descend on Oh-down.

Make sure the students are given enough time between phrases to act them out.

Side coach additional detail at any time.

TRYING ON CHARACTERS

Small children are natural imitators. They have enjoyed imitating mother, father, doctors, farmers, truck drivers, etc., since birth. As children get older they become more inhibited, making it important to try on characters.

Trying on characters is having the students become other persons, animals or objects. These roles require students to define and develop feelings and actions. It is the time to practice facial expressions, body postures, and rates of movement to show feelings. Also it gives the students an opportunity to experiment with and develop ideas for possible actions the characters/objects might be engaged in during a given situation. Details are needed to enhance character/object development and trying on characters helps to work them out. Furthermore, it's a time for you to side coach any suggestions you may have to facilitate the role since students will have a more limited frame of reference.

Trying on characters requires only as much time as the teacher decides to invest. This varies with the number of characters you've chosen to do and/or the number of times you redo a character to get the detail desired. And it's usually done at the students' desks, either standing or sitting.

Trying on characters can be used to prepare you and the students for a more involved creative drama activity such as role playing a complicated situation or story dramatization. Role playing situations and story dramatizations don't happen accidentally. By trying on characters these end products will fall into place with ease. TRY IT ON - YOU'LL LIKE IT!

To check story comprehension:

Show me
— something the main character did in today's story. (Recall)
— something else this character did. (Recall)
— (by using facial expressions) how this character looked when _____ happened. (Feelings)
— what you think will happen next. (Drawing Conclusions)
— how you think a character would react in some unrelated situation. (Inference)

To check listening and to add pleasure to story time (periodically pause):

Ask the students to show

— how a character feels. (Feelings)
— what they think will happen next. (Drawing Conclusions)
— how they think this character will react to a given situation. (Inference)

To develop characteristics of personalities or objects to be dramatized:

Try becoming

historical characters - Christopher Columbus, Paul Revere, Benjamin Franklin, George Washington.
occupations - fireman, doctor, teacher, bookkeeper, secretary, policeman, clerk.
objects - candle, snowman, tree, typewriter, toaster, percolator, sun, popcorn popper.
animals - elephant, giraffe, lion, dog, horse, bird, chicken, turtle, rabbit, cat.
types of people/emotions - an old person, a wicked witch, an angry taxi driver, a tired jogger, an elated track star, a sneaky sleuth, a frustrated teacher!

Trying on characters motivates and peaks student interest.

INTEGRATED
LESSONS

Using Creative Drama

The following lessons contain creative drama activities integrated into a variety of content areas. The drama portion of these lessons can be omitted and you'll still have a successful lesson. However, creative drama will enhance and firmly plant into the students' minds the concept you're teaching.

✳ Denotes the use of creative drama within the lesson.

⬤ Designates activity pages you are permitted to reproduce.

AREA: Science/Language Arts

TOPIC: Space/Point of View

OBJECTIVE: To increase the student's affective feelings toward science through creative drama. Through the integration of science and language arts, the students will write a point-of-view selection.

PROCEDURE:

1. Separately describe what qualities a robot/spaceperson possesses. List vocabulary if desirable.

*2. Have the children find a self-space and try on robot/spaceperson body movements. Have the students move about the room walking as a robot/spaceperson floating. The teacher suggests moving the arms and legs, turning, bending, reaching, etc.

*3. Teacher, with two instruments of contrasting short and long sounds (i.e. tamborine, xylophone), alternates striking these while students alternate robot/spaceperson (jerky/smooth, floating) patterns. Teacher may side coach movements, such as turning, bending, twisting, etc. Float them back to home base.

4. Introduce the idea of people owning robots. Teacher can role play or discuss with the class possible demands of, feelings toward, and care given to robots under human ownership. Discuss or role play the robots' reactions to them if they were to have feelings.

5. Have the students individually think about owning a robot. What would they ask it to do? What kind of care does it need? How will they treat it? How do they feel about that robot? What type of feeling do they have for the robot?

*6. Have students pair off and role play being a robot and owner.

7. Have children write paragraphs from the point of view of owning a robot.

8. Reverse roles; write the robot's point of view of his owner.

FOLLOW-UP ACTIVITIES:

1. Illustrate.
2. Check out latest information of robot activities.
3. Try movement to music, example: "Star Wars."

Elicit a list of vocabulary words.

Have the children find a self-space and try on robot and spaceperson body movements.

ROBOTPERSON	ACTIONS TO TRY ON	SPACEPERSON
jerky	rotating	wavy
pauses	pulling	floats
halting	pushing	glides
half turns	lifting	smooth
small steps	reaching	slow motion
geometric	turning	supple
precision	bending	
automatic	stooping	
confined/rigid	stretching	
repetition		

Expect expressions of positive and negative points of view.

I don't like my owner. I never get oiled or shined. I get orders and more orders, but never a thank you...

Not everyone is as lucky as I. My owner treats me with such kindness. I'm oiled, dusted, and spit shined regularly...

My robot is very dependable. When it's needed, it always comes through doing better than I expect. It cleans, cooks, dusts, and takes out the trash with great efficiency...

My robot is lazy. I try to be thoughtful and not nag, but that robot wouldn't do a thing if I didn't always keep checking up on it. There wouldn't be clean floors, clean chalkboards or...

24

ROBOT'S POINT OF VIEW

NOTION

CONVICTION

OWNER'S POINT OF VIEW

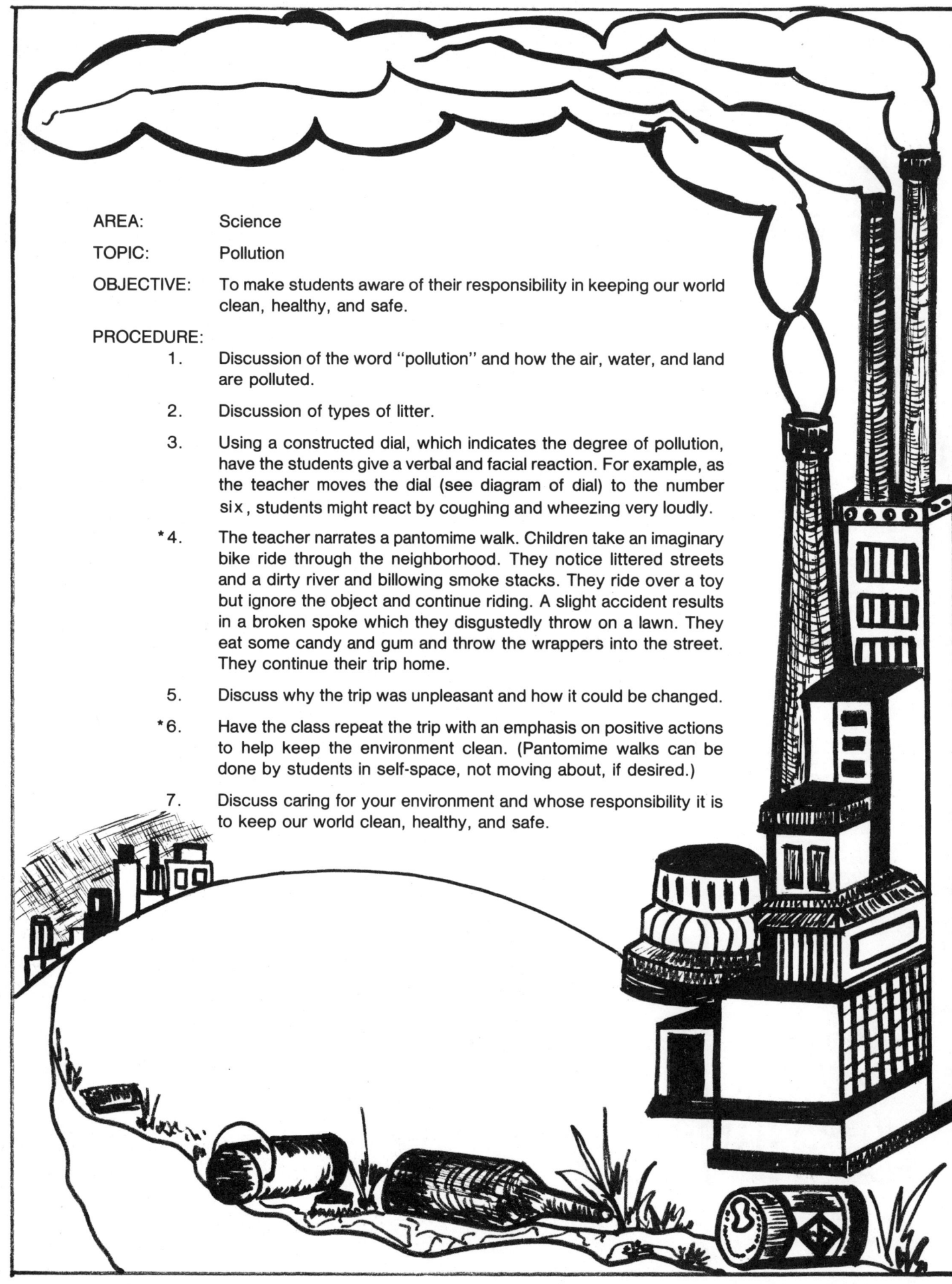

AREA: Science

TOPIC: Pollution

OBJECTIVE: To make students aware of their responsibility in keeping our world clean, healthy, and safe.

PROCEDURE:

1.   Discussion of the word "pollution" and how the air, water, and land are polluted.

2.   Discussion of types of litter.

3.   Using a constructed dial, which indicates the degree of pollution, have the students give a verbal and facial reaction. For example, as the teacher moves the dial (see diagram of dial) to the number six, students might react by coughing and wheezing very loudly.

*4.   The teacher narrates a pantomime walk. Children take an imaginary bike ride through the neighborhood. They notice littered streets and a dirty river and billowing smoke stacks. They ride over a toy but ignore the object and continue riding. A slight accident results in a broken spoke which they disgustedly throw on a lawn. They eat some candy and gum and throw the wrappers into the street. They continue their trip home.

5.   Discuss why the trip was unpleasant and how it could be changed.

*6.   Have the class repeat the trip with an emphasis on positive actions to help keep the environment clean. (Pantomime walks can be done by students in self-space, not moving about, if desired.)

7.   Discuss caring for your environment and whose responsibility it is to keep our world clean, healthy, and safe.

1. Class could clean up the playground.
2. Make pollution posters for their room and building.
3. List ways the class can help save our natural resources.
4. Do a before/after picture depicting effects of pollution.
5. Investigate the area - find concerns causing pollution - write a letter to the company stating your opinion.
6. Investigate animals that are endangered because of polluting and destroying of their homes.
7. Write a poem.
8. Make an advertisement promoting ecology and conservation.
9. Make a list of the causes of air pollution in your community.
10. Make a list of the different kinds of poison in the air.
11. Make a pamphlet that can be distributed in the neighborhood or as part of a school newspaper.
12. Invite a Public Health Service speaker to your school.
13. Have the Department of Natural Resources come and explain programs currently in operation in your area.

STOP! Take a look!
   Pollution is all around...
Have you recently checked
   your air, water and ground?
Smoke and fumes
   are being emitted from industrial plants.
Are we really giving
   the animals a fair chance?
Cars, boats, trains and planes
   have terrible exhausts.
If we don't act now
   all will be lost!
Incinerators burning garbage and refuse
   put fumes and smoke into the sky.
Action! Take action!
   Or all will wither and die.

For teacher use with a large group and/or individual student use.

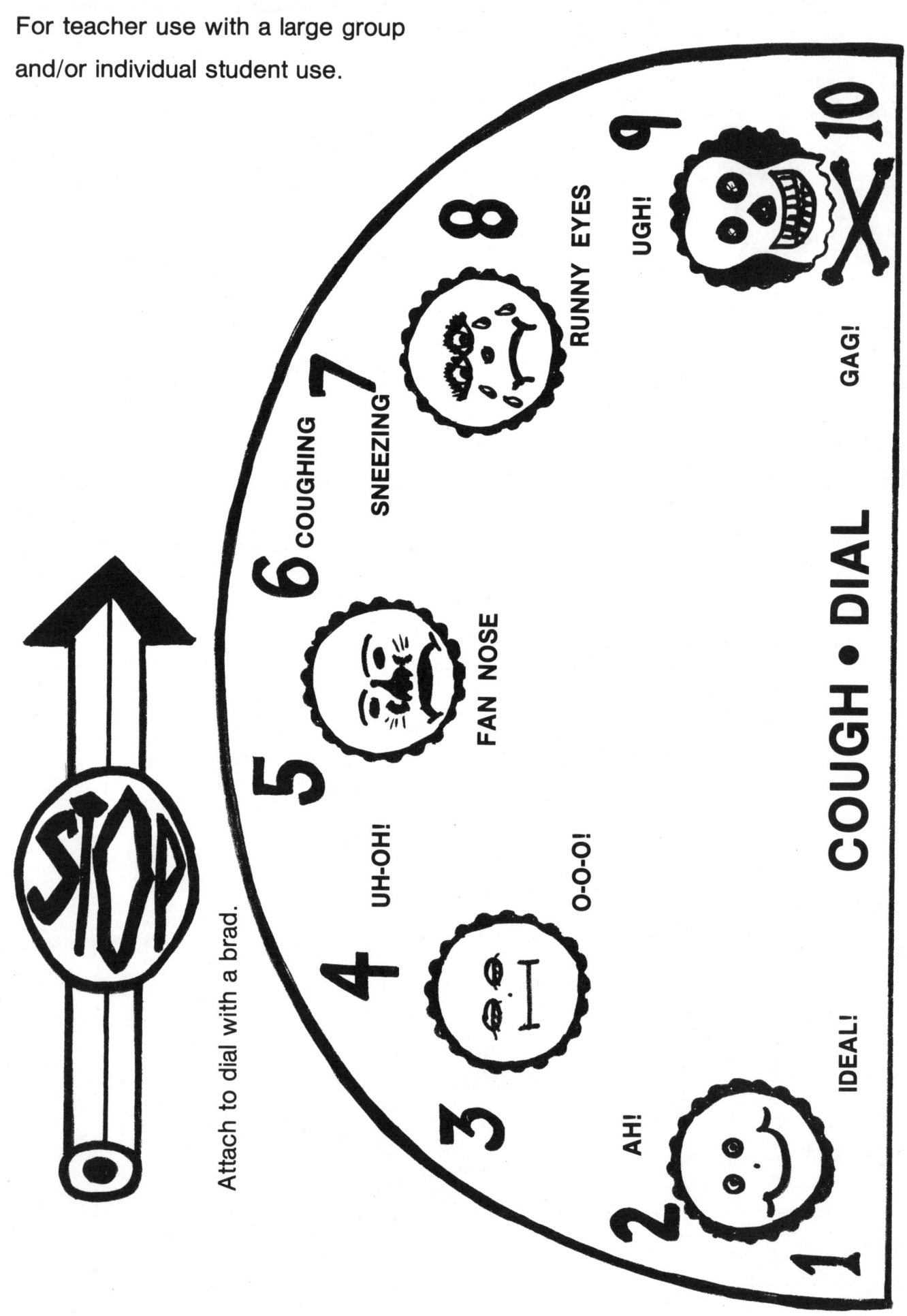

Attach to dial with a brad.

COUGH • DIAL

1
2 AH! IDEAL!
3 UH-OH!
4
5 FAN NOSE O-O-O!
6 COUGHING
7 SNEEZING
8 RUNNY EYES
9 UGH!
10 GAG!

STOP

28

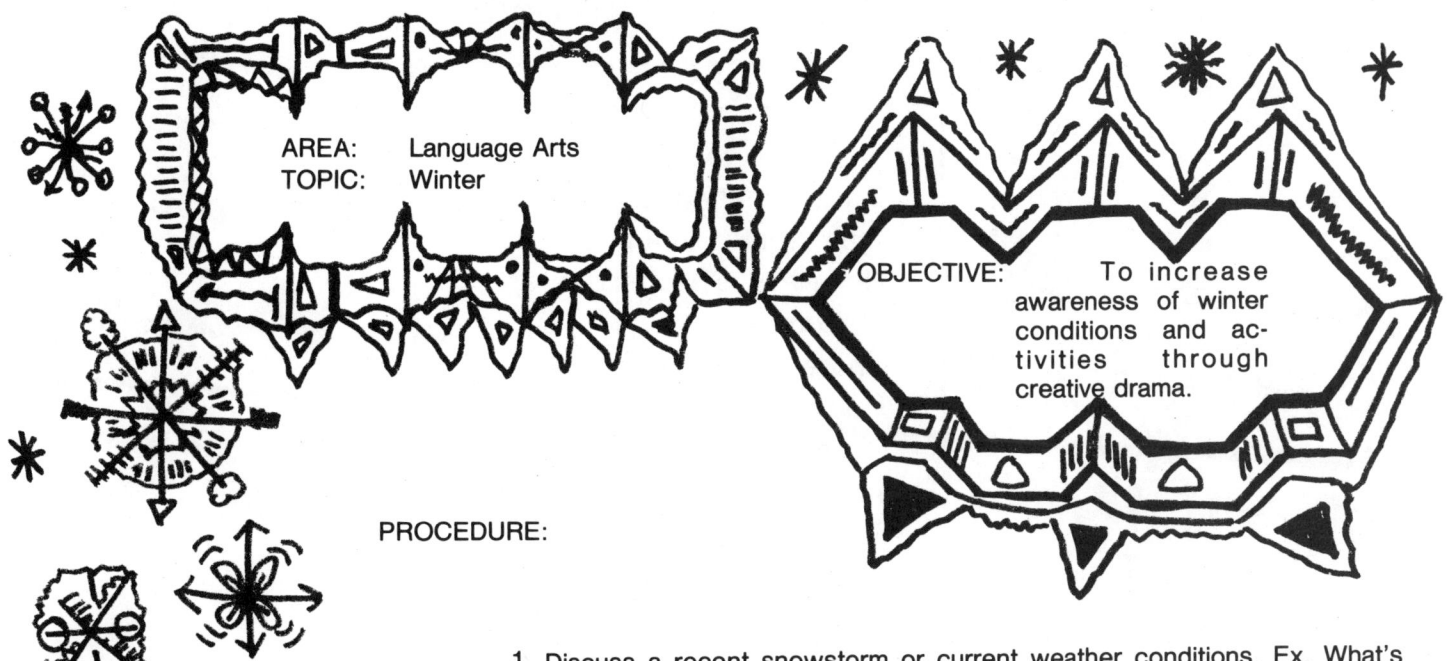

AREA: Language Arts
TOPIC: Winter

OBJECTIVE: To increase awareness of winter conditions and activities through creative drama.

PROCEDURE:

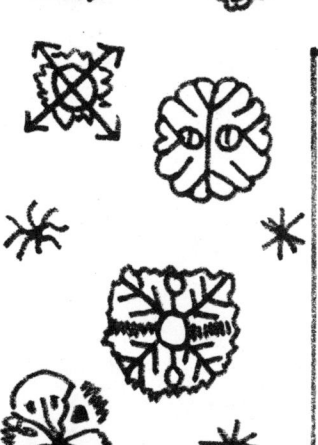

1. Discuss a recent snowstorm or current weather conditions. Ex. What's happening here? What's happening in Florida, California and other parts of the country? (Or imagine you are in a part of our country where you could do this.)
2. Elicit from the children what they like to do on a snowy day, for example, sledding, skating, skiing, throwing snowballs, making snowmen or forts.
3. Discuss how to build a snowman and what is needed.
4. Read the snowman poem.
*5. Have the children find a space of their own in the room. Following the side coaching from the teacher, each child builds an imaginary snowman.
   a. Make a snowball, lay it down carefully and roll the base of the snowman.
   b. Repeat for middle and head, making them the appropriate sizes.
   c. Exaggerate the weight and chore of lifting them into place.
   d. After decorating and dressing the snowman, evaluate how it looks, adjusting a lumpy side or crooked hat.
*6. Each child steps inside and "becomes" that snowman. The children act out the poem as the teacher narrates. (The teacher pauses in reading to suggest actions.)
*7. While students are still in position, evaluate, discuss and practice changes that could be made, for example, how to move as a snowman, how to open the door and go inside, how to melt slowly to the floor.
*8. Repeat the poem and pantomime.

FOLLOW-UP ACTIVITIES:
   1. Write an individual or class winter poem and illustrate.
   2. Write a winter story and illustrate.
   3. Write a paragraph from the snowman's point of view describing the weather or the children. Do the point of view of the children toward the weather or snowman.
   4. Draw a winter action scene.
   5. Make a mural, mobile, or diorama.
   6. Make a chart of the weather conditions for a week.
   7. Go to the playground and build a snowman.
   8. Sing winter songs.

Cars splash me.
Look! I'm muddy!
Ouch! That hurts.
My eyes don't match.
Don't hit so hard.
Look at that lump.
I'm so perfectly round!

Once a magical snowman
Was created in a park.
He loved his hand-me-down
  clothes
And every friendly remark.
He would run, jump, skip
  and play,
And hoped it'd never
  get dark.

Soon the sun will shine
  down strong,
His hat will slip, slide and
  fall.
He will melt and shrink
  in size
No longer agile and tall.
Then only a remaining
  puddle
Will show he existed at all.

They're strangling me!
Only dogs come and
  visit...
Kids stop and chat!
I lost a button.
I have a stiff neck!
Ouch! That snowball
  hurt!

Possible discussion questions to use prior to the writing assignment on the next page:

1. Does it matter where you put your snowman?

2. How might it feel about its shape?

3. Does it like the way you dressed it?

4. How does it feel about how you put its face on and what you used?

5. Do you think it might be lonely?

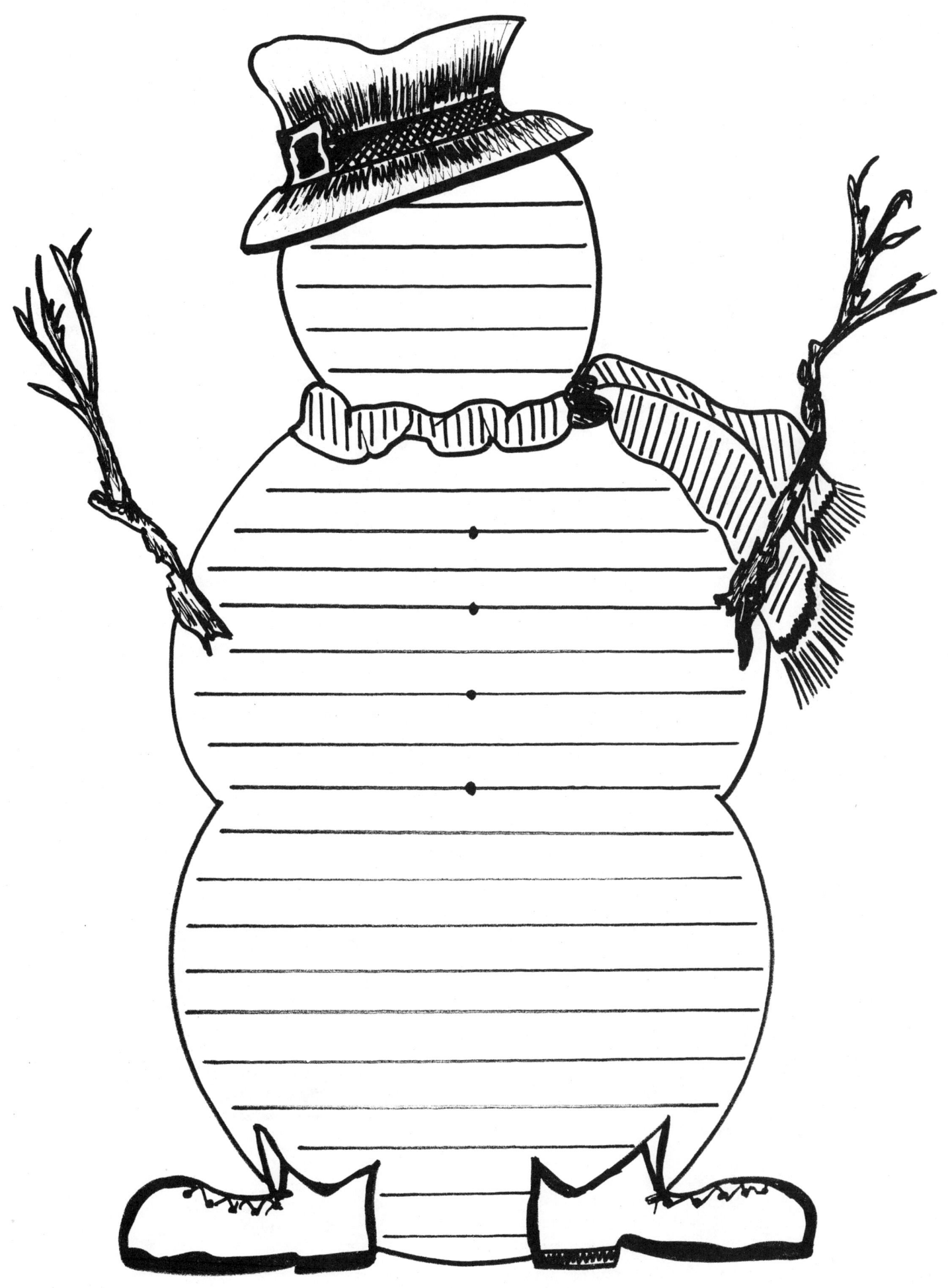

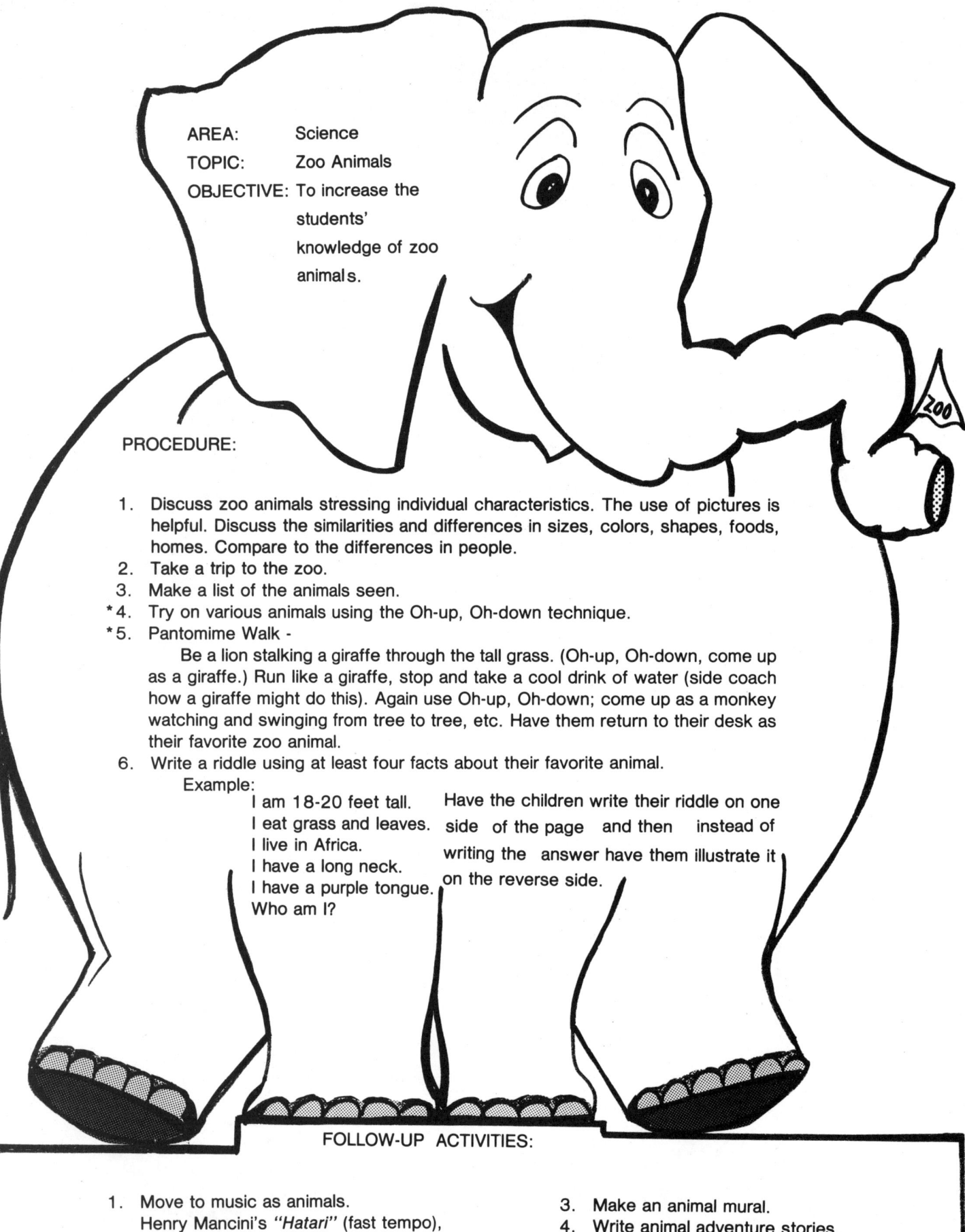

AREA: Science

TOPIC: Zoo Animals

OBJECTIVE: To increase the students' knowledge of zoo animals.

PROCEDURE:

1. Discuss zoo animals stressing individual characteristics. The use of pictures is helpful. Discuss the similarities and differences in sizes, colors, shapes, foods, homes. Compare to the differences in people.
2. Take a trip to the zoo.
3. Make a list of the animals seen.
*4. Try on various animals using the Oh-up, Oh-down technique.
*5. Pantomime Walk -
   Be a lion stalking a giraffe through the tall grass. (Oh-up, Oh-down, come up as a giraffe.) Run like a giraffe, stop and take a cool drink of water (side coach how a giraffe might do this). Again use Oh-up, Oh-down; come up as a monkey watching and swinging from tree to tree, etc. Have them return to their desk as their favorite zoo animal.
6. Write a riddle using at least four facts about their favorite animal.
   Example:

   I am 18-20 feet tall.
   I eat grass and leaves.
   I live in Africa.
   I have a long neck.
   I have a purple tongue.
   Who am I?

   Have the children write their riddle on one side of the page and then instead of writing the answer have them illustrate it on the reverse side.

FOLLOW-UP ACTIVITIES:

1. Move to music as animals.
   Henry Mancini's *"Hatari"* (fast tempo),
   "Baby Elephant Walk" (slow tempo)
2. Make papier-maché animals.
3. Make an animal mural.
4. Write animal adventure stories.
5. Write a report.

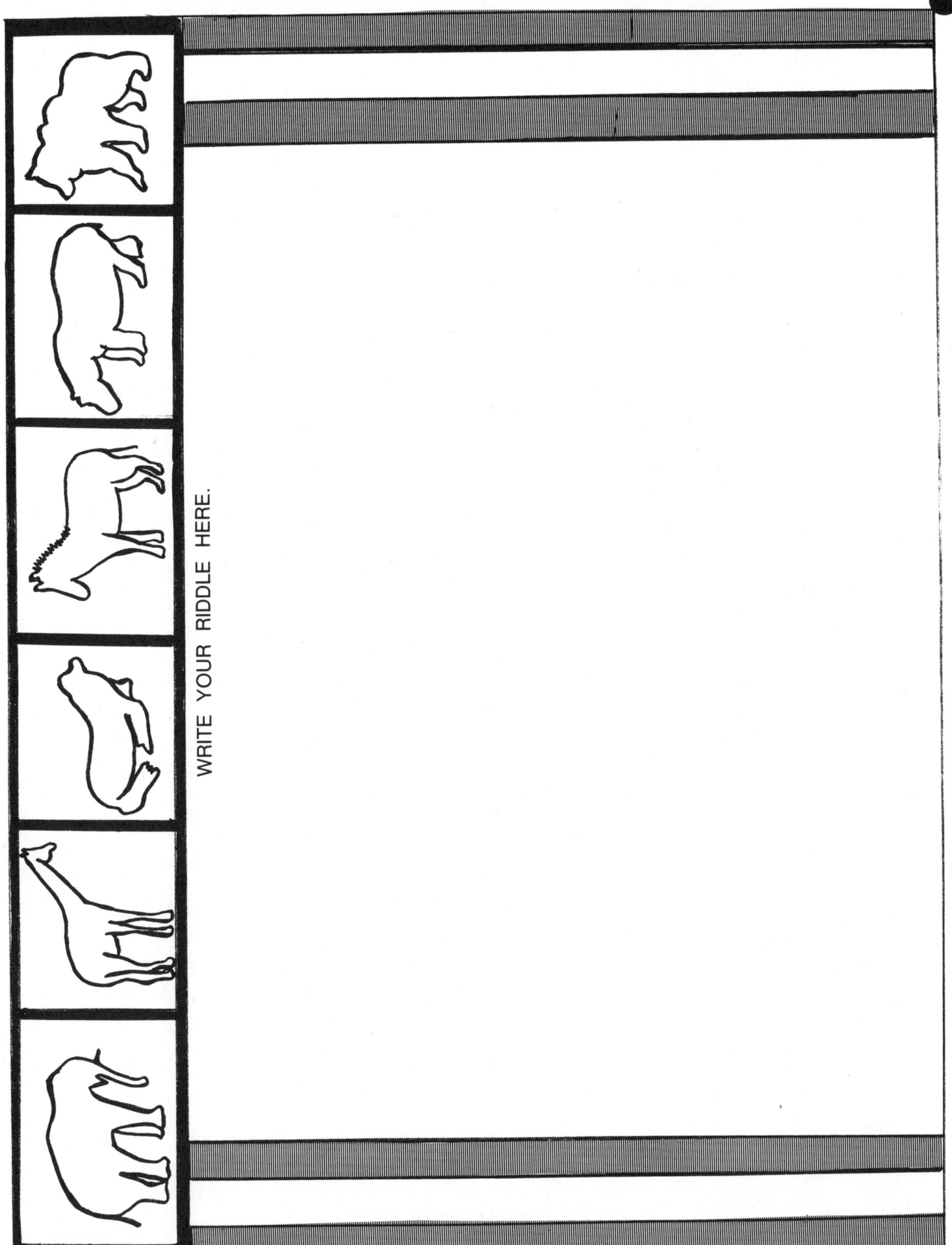

WRITE YOUR RIDDLE HERE.

AREA: Science

TOPIC: Plants

OBJECTIVE: To understand the types of plant propagation and stages of growth.

PROCEDURE:

1. Discuss the different types of plant propagation - cuttings, seed, bulbs, etc.

2. Planting:

   a. Fall - Find a place on school property to "beautify" (the principal will love it!). Have each child plant a specific number of bulbs (crocus, daffodil, or tulip bulbs work nicely).

   b. Spring - Again using school property, plant seeds. Vegetables or flowers would work.

   c. Winter - Plant seeds in flats or individual styrofoam cups.

   NOTE: In the fall the kids worked hard and were very excited when done. However, the greatest excitement and pride came in the spring when the flowers came up.

3. Recall with the class all of the things they had done so far -the selection of seeds, tilling, cleaning up and leveling of soil, plotting, digging and planting, cleaning up.

4. Discuss and predict what might happen and how the plants will grow. At this point you may wish to show a movie/filmstrip on plant growth.

*5. Have each child find a self-space in the room:

   a. Pantomime (teacher side coaches) the getting ready and planting process.

   b. Have each child "become" that seed or bulb he planted. Have him "grow" for you. A good way to set the pace of growth is for the teacher to set it using the beat of a drum or tambourine.

6. Complete the Activity Sheet provided.

FOLLOW-UP ACTIVITIES:

1. Chart and graph the actual growth of their plants.

2. Write a poem or story.

WRITE THE STEPS OF PLANTING. THE PICTURES WILL HELP YOU.

choice
of seed
or bulb

getting
ready

planting

care

LUCKY! *Fortunately, I got a new bike.*

AREA: Language Arts

TOPIC: Sequencing/Creative Writing

OBJECTIVE: Through the use of creative drama the students will have a greater awareness of the sequential development of a story and be able to write one.

PROCEDURE:

1. Read the story "Fortunately" by Remy Charlip.

2. Clarify the meanings of the words **fortunately** and **unfortunately** by having the students give synonyms.

3. Recall the purpose and the order of events in the story.

4. Using the fortunately statements from the story, solicit several alternative unfortunately statements.

5. Give other examples of fortunately statements and have students respond with unfortunately statements.

*6. The class takes a Pantomime Walk while the teacher narrates the story. (See next page.)

7. Using a prescribed destination (for example, going to the store, a football game, skiing, a canoe trip), the children will verbally develop a similar story.

8. Discuss the need for a sequential progression within the story so that it reaches a conclusion.

9. Complete the suggested follow-up page. (Optional)

10. Have each child write and illustrate his own Fortunately/Unfortunately story.

FOLLOW-UP ACTIVITIES:

1. Share students' stories with each other.

2. Share their stories with another class.

Unfortunately, it had a flat tire.

UNLUCKY!

Note to the Teacher: After you take the walk have each child (or as many as you want) pantomime what he/she bought while the others guess.

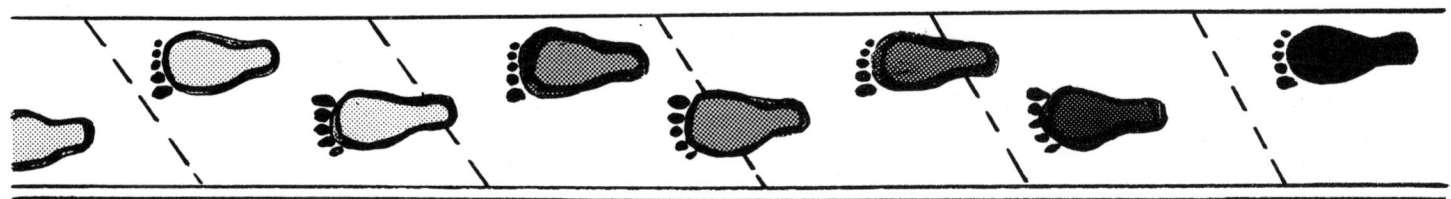

Pantomime Walk

Find a space of your own in the room...make sure no one is real close to you... O.K., here we go...It's Saturday. You decide to visit a friend...Go to the closet... get your coat...put it on...get your hat...Do you really need it? No...put it back... go to the front door, open it...close it...start walking to your friend's house...You have to cross the street...look both ways...O.K. Cross... There's the house...Go up to the door...Knock, wait...Knock again...I guess no one's home...Turn around ...back down the street...Look! There's something in the bushes...Bend over, pick it up...IT'S A DOLLAR BILL! YES!! Lucky you!...Now, what can you do with it?...You decide you're going to go to the dime store to buy something...Start walking to the store...show the people around you, by the way you walk, how happy you are and how lucky you feel...Here's the store...Open the door...walk in...Oops, you forgot to close the door...make sure you closed it tight. Good... Start looking...Go up and down the aisles. Oh, that looks nice...Pick it up, check the price...Too much...Put it back...Walk again...turn the corner...down another aisle...There's something. Pick it up...No, it doesn't look as nice as you thought it would...There's just what you want...Pick it up...Look it over very carefully... Check it for scratches, dents or holes...It looks good...take it to to the cashier... pay for it...Don't forget your change...Go to the door...open it...close the door... Now, very happily walk back home (to their seats or some other designated area)

FORTUNATELY, _____
_____

UNFORTUNATELY, _____
_____

Directions: Write and draw a picture of a fortunately sentence. Next, trade papers with a friend. Read his fortunately sentence. Now write an unfortunately sentence to go with his and draw a picture. Remember to do a nice neat picture for your friend.

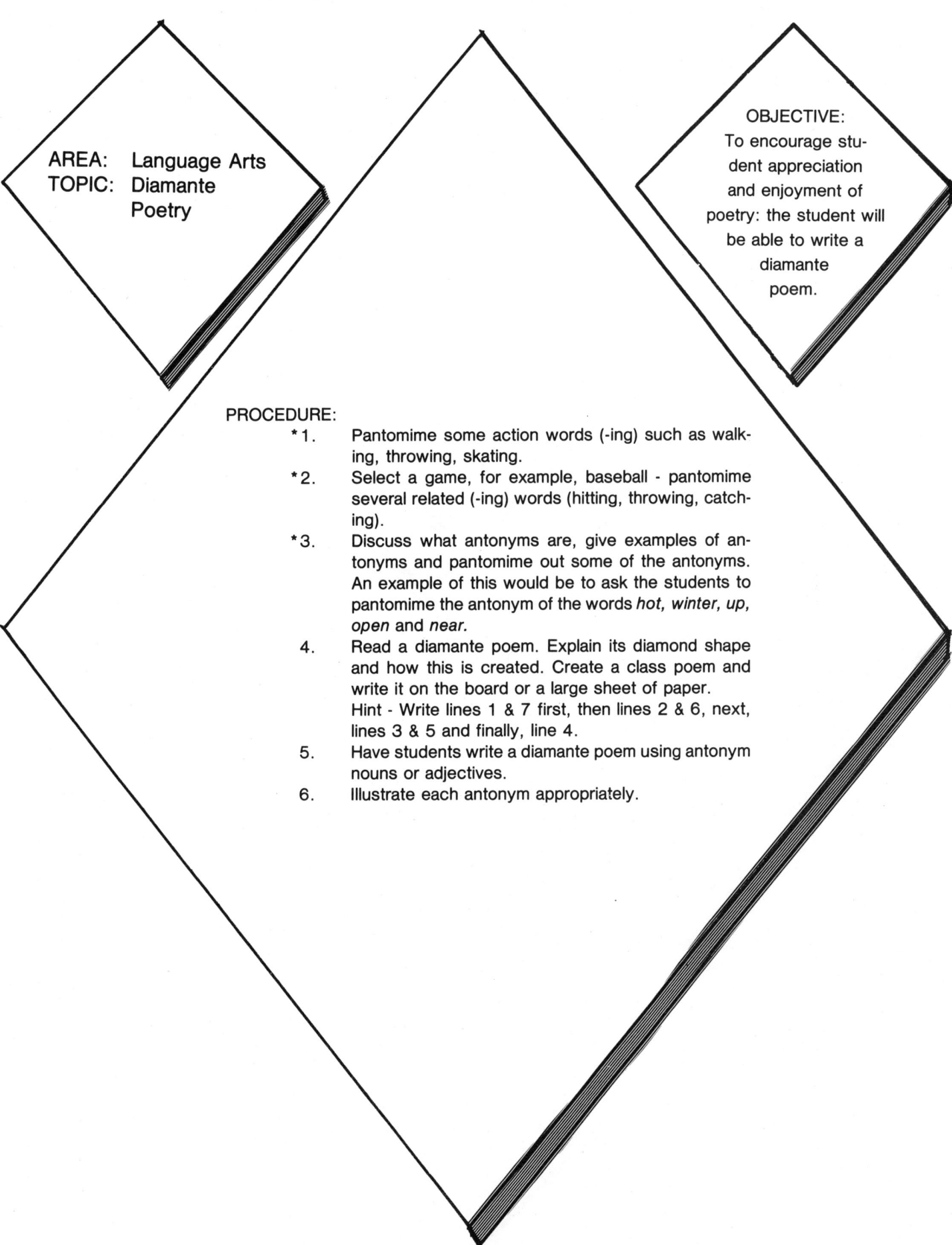

AREA: Language Arts
TOPIC: Diamante Poetry

OBJECTIVE:
To encourage student appreciation and enjoyment of poetry: the student will be able to write a diamante poem.

PROCEDURE:

*1. Pantomime some action words (-ing) such as walking, throwing, skating.

*2. Select a game, for example, baseball - pantomime several related (-ing) words (hitting, throwing, catching).

*3. Discuss what antonyms are, give examples of antonyms and pantomime out some of the antonyms. An example of this would be to ask the students to pantomime the antonym of the words *hot, winter, up, open* and *near*.

4. Read a diamante poem. Explain its diamond shape and how this is created. Create a class poem and write it on the board or a large sheet of paper.
Hint - Write lines 1 & 7 first, then lines 2 & 6, next, lines 3 & 5 and finally, line 4.

5. Have students write a diamante poem using antonym nouns or adjectives.

6. Illustrate each antonym appropriately.

39

DIAMANTE (dee-ah-mahn-tay)

Diamante is seven lines of contrasting ideas using specific parts
of speech.

Describes noun
on line 1.

Describes noun
on line 7.

NOUN (antonym)
ADJECTIVE, ADJECTIVE
VERB, (-ing or -ed), VERB, VERB
NOUN, NOUN IIII NOUN, NOUN
VERB, (-ing or -ed), VERB, VERB
ADJECTIVE, ADJECTIVE
NOUN (antonym)

FRIEND
KIND, THOUGHTFUL
LAUGHING, TALKING, SHARING
FAITHFUL, PAL, BULLY, DISLIKABLE
JEERING, YELLING, UNFEELING
MEAN, HORRIBLE
ENEMY

BASEBALL
EXCITEMENT, SWIFT
THROWING, CATCHING, HITTING
BAT, GLOVE, HELMET, PADS
PASSING, RECEIVING, RUNNING
ROUGH, STRENUOUS
FOOTBALL

DAY
WARM, BRIGHT
RUNNING, GIGGLING, PLAYING
MARVELOUS, SUN, MOON, SHADOWS
REACHING, CREEPING, SNEAKING
MYSTERIOUS, DARK
NIGHT

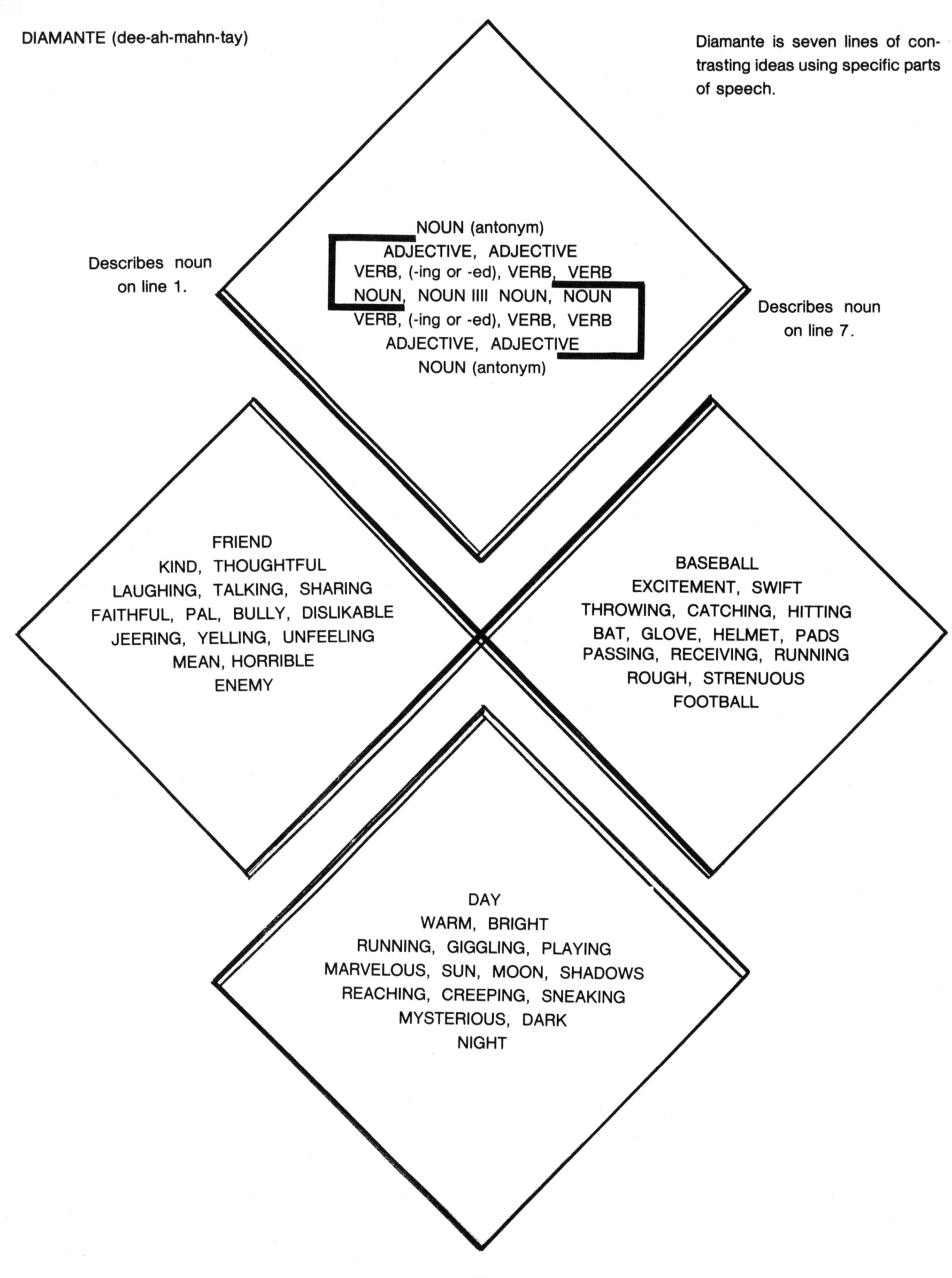

D I A M A N T E
(The Diamond)

Write a diamante poem and illustrate both antonyms.

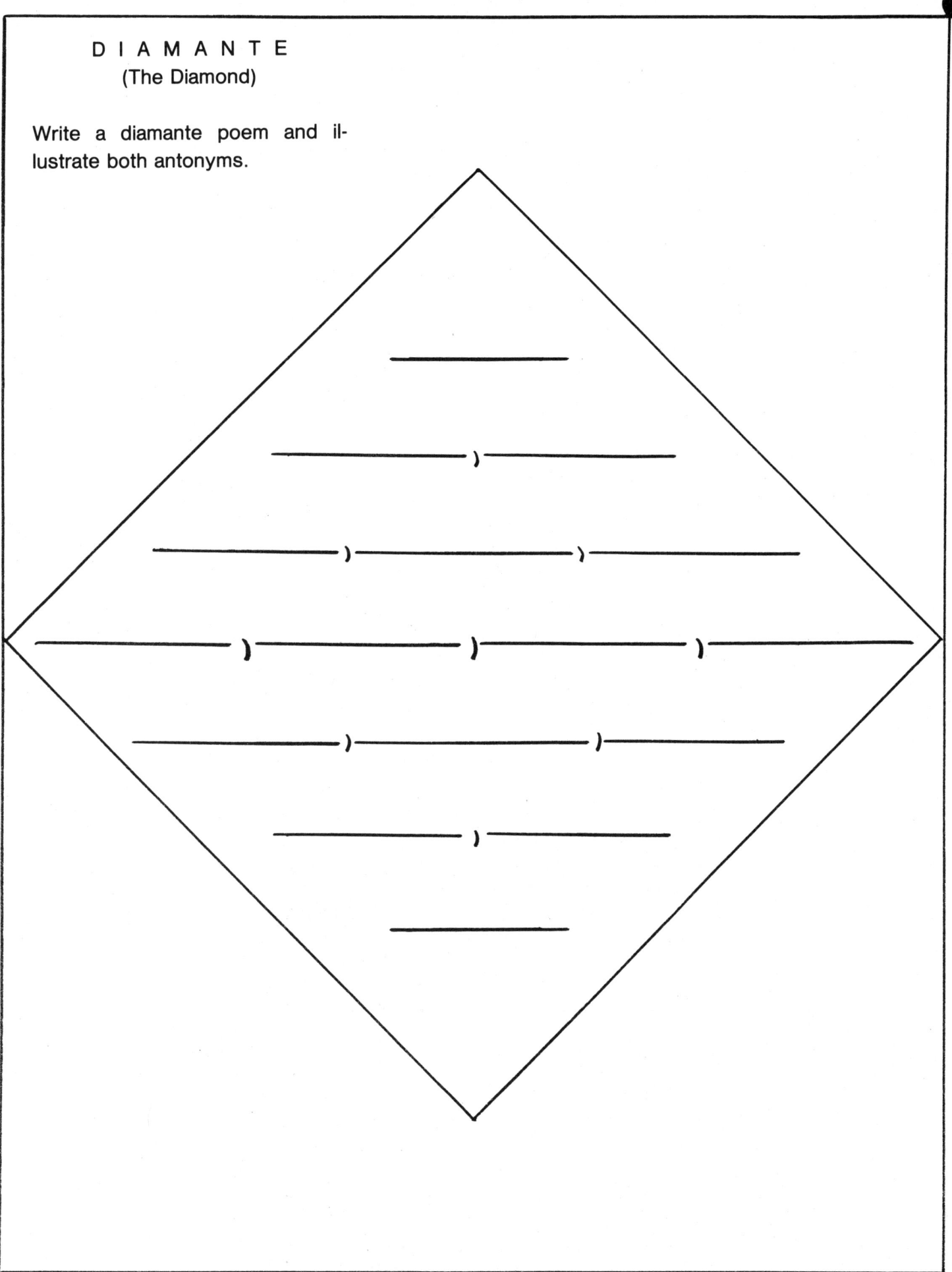

AREA: Math
TOPIC: Recipe

PROCEDURE:

OBJECTIVE:

Each student will
create a recipe.

1. Discuss where the students buy their ice-cream
    cones and what their favorite flavors are.
2. Elicit the steps involved in buying an ice-cream
    cone: arriving, entering the shop, looking,
    deciding, ordering, watching, taking the cone,
    paying, licking, eating the cone...

*3. Find a self-space and pantomime all or part of the process of buying the
     ice-cream cone. Side coach as they mime; be specific.
     Deciding on a hot summer day - look at the various flavors, change
     their minds, change their minds again, finally decide, wait their turn to
     order, give order. Stress exact actions: how they'd stand, move,
     shift their weight, feel, look around, move their heads, point, etc.
4.   Elicit possible ice-cream accompaniments and list on the board (whipping
     cream, chopped nuts, cherries, shaved coconut, cookies, bananas, etc.).

*5. Role play the worker in an ice-cream shop making a favorite dish of ice
     cream: get the dish, get and prepare each ingredient in order of use (peel
     bananas, unwrap a cookie, scoop the ice cream, drizzle the toppings,
     squirt the whipping cream, sprinkle the nuts, place the cherry). Then,
     carry it to a place to sit and begin to eat it (probably at their desks).
6.   Have each student create a dream dish of ice cream and illustrate (see
     Recipe Sheet on next page). The dream dish explanation should give the
     order in which the ingredients are used and how (scooped, plopped,
     drizzled, etc.).
     Note — Try to keep the students realistic in that 90 scoops of ice
     cream would not serve 9 people but probably would serve 45-90,
     depending upon how many scoops per person.

FOLLOW-UP ACTIVITIES:
1. Design a poster to advertise this newly created master-
    piece!
2. Make sundaes.
3. Make up money math problems.

Write a recipe for a fantastic ice-cream dish. Tell its name, how many it serves, and how much of each ingredient is needed (specify flavors). Then write an explanation of how it's constructed. Tell what you do and the order in which it's done.

SPECIALTY:

SERVES:

CREATED BY:

INGREDIENTS:

EXPLANATION:

AREA: Language Arts/Reading

TOPIC: Point of View

OBJECTIVE: To become aware of and understand point of view. Each student will write a story using point of view.

PROCEDURE:
1. Read Grimm's fairy tale *Hansel and Gretel.*
2. Discuss and recall the order of events.
*3. Try-on Characters:
   Witch - Facial expressions, how her hands would move, how she would walk, sit down, hold her body and speak.
   Hansel and Gretel - Show their actions and feelings while leaving their home, laying their path, and approaching the witch's house and sampling it.
*4. Act out scenes:
   a. Father and Stepmother discussing why they can't care for them any longer while Hansel listens.
   b. Hansel and Gretel laying out their path.
   c. The discovery and eating of the Gingerbread House.
   d. Their first encounter with the witch.
   e. The lockup of the children.
   f. The children's escape.
5. Set the scenes.
*6. Recap the story while players enact it (pausing for action and dialog).
7. Evaluate with the class what they liked, disliked and how they would change it if done again.

8. Discussion:
   a. How do you think the witch felt when she discovered the children tearing her house apart?
   b. If you had been the witch what would you have done?
   c. Are all witches wicked? (ex. Good Witch in *The Wizard of Oz*)
9. Introduction of point of view:

   Point of view requires looking at a situation from a different perspective. A way of doing this with Hansel and Gretel is to have the class imagine that the witch's motives had been misunderstood and her actions misinterpreted by the children.
10. Read "The Witch's Tale."
11. Have each child choose a fairy tale he is extremely familiar with. After choosing one of the characters, have each child write a story using that character's point of view expressing his/her/its interpretations and experiences.

STORY	POINT OF VIEW
The Three Little Pigs	Wolf
Little Red Riding Hood	Grandmother, Wolf, Woodsman
Jack and the Beanstalk	Giant
Three Billy Goats Gruff	Troll
Goldilocks	Bears

FOLLOW-UP ACTIVITIES:
1. Make a class storybook.
2. Illustrate their story.
3. Do more point-of-view writing.

The Witch's Tale

Who's there?

One day while I was cleaning my fireplace, getting ready to make a brew, I heard a tapping noise coming from outside. I was tempted to open the door but decided to look out the window instead. There were two bedraggled kids pulling my house apart and eating it.

I felt sorry for them. They looked poor and hungry. I invited them in to share my stew. After we ate we read some books by the nice warm fireplace. I invited them to stay for the night. That night, while lying in bed, I realized I was still upset about the damage they'd caused to my house and the possible expense of repairing it. I decided to overlook it for now.

The next morning as we ate breakfast I learned that they had no place to go. I offered to have them stay on with me as long as they were willing to help with the chores.

Things went along well for about three weeks. Hansel kept the little shed cleaned, fed the animals and pulled weeds in the garden. Gretel helped me bring in the wood, fix the food and wash the dishes.

One day we decided to have a party. While I was preparing the food, the fire started to sputter and smoke. Gretel was busy so I leaned over to check it. As I did, I felt someone push me. I fell forward into the fire, and while struggling to get to my feet again, I heard Gretel running and calling to her brother. I hoped she was going for help.

Gretel never returned and Hansel disappeared, too. Later I was more saddened when I discovered some of my most prized pieces of jewelry missing. I had enjoyed their company and it's still difficult for me to understand how all of that could have happened.

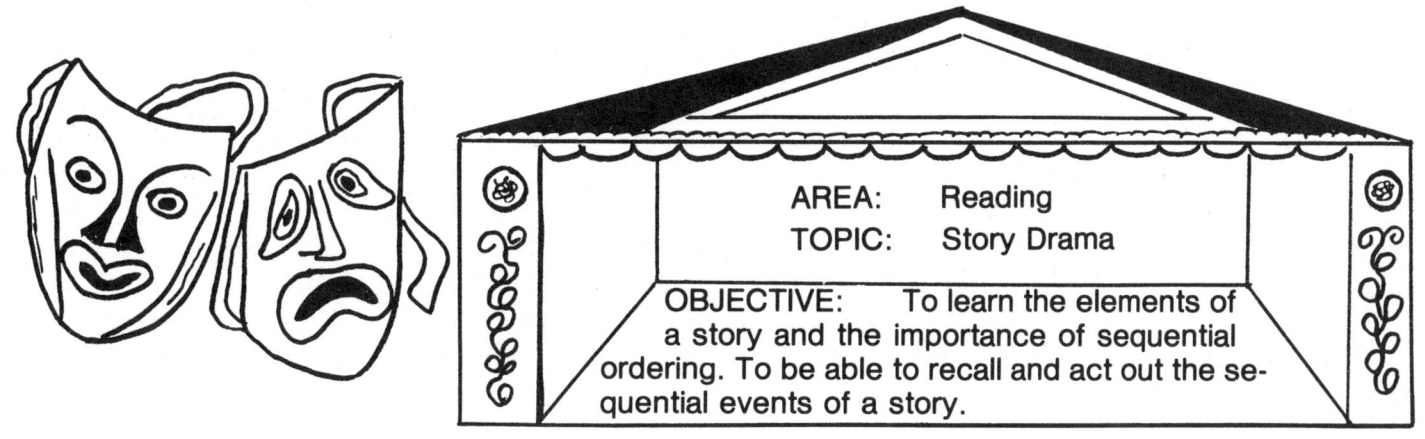

AREA: Reading
TOPIC: Story Drama

OBJECTIVE: To learn the elements of a story and the importance of sequential ordering. To be able to recall and act out the sequential events of a story.

PROCEDURE:

1. Discuss the importance of sequential order of events in directions, recipes, stories, etc.

*2. Have the students warm up by giving four sequential directions to the class; the class must act out the directions. Example: Everyone stand up, hit your thighs 3 times, clap your hands 3 times, sit down.

3. Select a story they are familiar with. Have the students recall the order of events. Discuss and identify the element of a story - the setting, main characters, events, climax and ending or resolution.

4. Read a story to the class. An example might be "Stone Soup" by Marcia Joan Brown. Have the students recall and identify the elements of the story and sequence the order of events. List them on the board.

*5. Have the students try on characters from the story. Each student needs to find a self-space. Have them act like hungry tired soldiers, frightened suspicious peasants, a strict mayor, and a kind, reverent priest. Give suggestions for expressions and movements.

*6. Role play: Have students volunteer or use the whole class to show soldiers begging for food, soldiers making soup in a big pot and adding different ingredients, setting a table, eating and drinking.

7. Set the scenes: Designate in the room the road to the village, the main street in the town, the peasant's house and a village square.

*8. Review the events and then ask for volunteers to play the characters. Walk them through the events while the teacher narrates. Discuss the additional movements, reactions and expressions that can be added. Try it again with changes and added verbal dialogue from the students.

9. Optional - Students can create their own story making sure it contains all the elements of a good story.

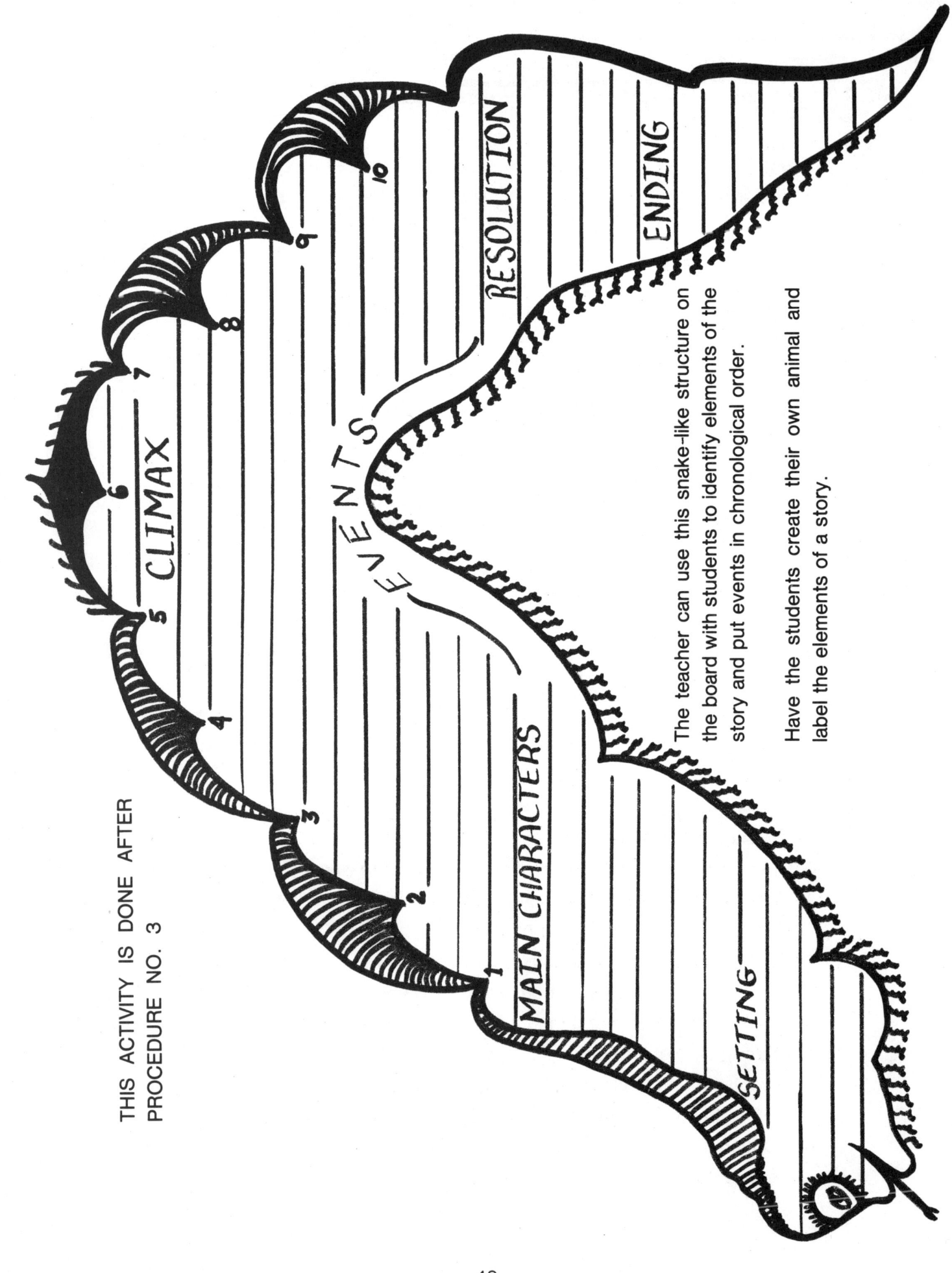

THIS ACTIVITY IS DONE AFTER PROCEDURE NO. 3

MAIN CHARACTERS

SETTING

EVENTS

CLIMAX

RESOLUTION

ENDING

The teacher can use this snake-like structure on the board with students to identify elements of the story and put events in chronological order.

Have the students create their own animal and label the elements of a story.

48

AREA: Language Arts/Reading

TOPIC: Idioms/Figurative Language

OBJECTIVE: To increase the awareness and understanding of idioms/figurative language.

SHE WAS ON TOP OF THE WORLD WHEN SHE WON THE TROPHY!

PROCEDURE:

1. Briefly explain and discuss idioms.
2. Demonstrate a pantomime of an idiomatic expression. Following the mime, use the idiom in context and discuss its correct meaning. Repeat its use in context to be sure the meaning is understood.
    Suggestion: Pantomime the large words one at a time indicating correct guesses by the class. Then do another word of the idiom until they've guessed or nearly guessed the idiom.
3. Repeat Step 2 as many times as you wish.
*4. Pantomiming by the students.
    a. Distribute the prepared cards to volunteer students.
    b. Have the student act out the words in the idiom.
    c. Have the student read the sentence on the reverse side of the card to the class.
    d. Teacher and students discuss the idiom's meaning.
    e. Give other sentences using the same idiom to clarify its meaning.
    f. Repeat these steps for each card.
       Hints:
       1) The presenter should indicate when ready to start and a correct response by pointing or repeating it.
       2) Side coach and encourage students when needed: try it another way, re-emphasizing miming one word at a time, encourage presenter to listen to the audience, encourage audience to allow pauses as presenter changes words, call time if necessary.
5. Distribute a list of idioms to the class. Read it together and discuss any that may need an explanation.
6. Write sentences using idioms and sufficient explanation showing that the idioms' meanings are clear.
7. Students choose one sentence to write and illustrate on a separate piece of drawing paper to be displayed or clipped into a booklet for sharing.

HE WAS UP A CREEK WITHOUT A PADDLE... BECAUSE HIS HOMEWORK WASN'T DONE.

49

IDIOMATIC EXPRESSIONS

let the cat out of the bag
up a creek without a paddle
foot in the mouth
his hands are tied
for the birds
count noses
hit the ceiling
keep your nose to the grindstone
eyes bigger than his stomach
ball of fire
pain in the neck
keep your eyes on the board
look before you leap
hollow leg
walked away with
hit the jackpot
beating his brains out
have to face the music
on pins and needles
talking through his hat
feather in your cap
ray of sunshine
blowing his own horn
hang in there
snowed under
in a pickle
his face fell
put her foot down
looking for a needle in a haystack
blows her money
out of sorts

TO GET AN IDEA I HAD TO
PUT ON MY THINKING CAP!

let it slip through her fingers
raining cats and dogs
climbing the walls
green thumb
put on your thinking caps
had his hands full
jump at the chance
turn over a new leaf
buttering up someone
go to bat for others
walking on air
on the right track
buckle down
held up
on his toes
rolled out the red carpet
over the hump
in a dog's age
down in the dumps
all thumbs
look a gift horse in the mouth
apple of her eye
stick your neck out
bury the hatchet
behind his back
get a kick out of
hit the nail on the head
stole the show
running around in circles
jumped out of my skin
all the same to me

TRYING TO FIND A PENCIL IN MY DESK IS
LIKE FINDING A NEEDLE IN A HAYSTACK!

Cut out and use with Step 4a of the lesson plan. It may be desirable to plastic coat these individual cards.

IDIOM	IDIOM	IDIOM
-walked away with	-on his toes	-on the right track
IDIOM	IDIOM	IDIOM
-jump at the chance	-hang around	-pick out
IDIOM	IDIOM	IDIOM
-at your fingertips	-count noses	-hit the ceiling
IDIOM	IDIOM	IDIOM
-fell off	-held up	-hollow leg
IDIOM	IDIOM	IDIOM
-let the cat out of the bag	-put on your thinking caps	-had his hands full
IDIOM	IDIOM	IDIOM
-fed up	-at large	-put her foot in her mouth

SENTENCE	SENTENCE	SENTENCE
You're on the right track and should soon have the problem solved.	Jim had to be on his toes to get more butterflies than Sam.	Sara walked away with several bowling trophies.
SENTENCE	SENTENCE	SENTENCE
Pick out the one you like and try it on.	They were planning to hang around the park after the game.	David would jump at the chance to go roller-skating.
SENTENCE	SENTENCE	SENTENCE
My brother is going to hit the ceiling when he finds out I lost his football.	The teacher had to count noses to be sure everyone was on the bus.	Do you have that information at your fingertips?
SENTENCE	SENTENCE	SENTENCE
He has a hollow leg when it comes to eating ice cream.	The crossing guard held up traffic until the children had crossed the street.	The club's attendance fell off when the weather was rainy.
SENTENCE	SENTENCE	SENTENCE
The baby sitter had his hands full watching the three small children.	All right, put on your thinking caps and see how many other words you can think of.	Everyone knew about the surprise party because Tom had let the cat out of the bag.
SENTENCE	SENTENCE	SENTENCE
Susan had problems with her sister because she frequently put her foot in her mouth.	The animals were allowed to roam at large.	I'm fed up with this rainy weather.

AREA: Language Arts/Reading

TOPIC: Mystery Story Elements/Sequencing

OBJECTIVE: To develop an increased appreciation of mystery stories and their elements.

PROCEDURE:

1. Read "The Case of Sir Biscuit-Shooter" from *Encyclopedia Brown Solves Them All* by Donald Sobol to the class.

2. Discuss which type of mystery story this is, detection or supernatural.

3. Discuss the elements of a mystery as they are used: the excitement, the clues, the mystery or crime, the method of detection, and suspense.

*4. Do a story drama, one scene at a time:

   a. Recall the characters and sequence the scene with the students.

   b. Try on some characters and decide who is portraying each character needed.

   c. Decide upon the location in the classroom for this scene.

   d. Stress staying in character.

   e. Read or recap the action and story line for that portion of the story as the students act it out.

   f. Students could spontaneously verbalize as part of their staying in character.

   g. You may want to evaluate with the students what just took place, practice special movements that might improve it, and have the students redo the scene with/without the narration.

*5. With the scenes located in different areas of the classroom, you can go through the story drama in its entirety without interruptions.

6. Add any details you feel will enhance the story drama. Suggestions: At the circus you could have a ticket taker, a barker, more people in the audience, a popcorn seller, a ringmaster, several acts in the ring such as the strong man, the bareback rider, the lion tamer and the sword swallower.

7. Have the students select a mystery story to read and do a book report.

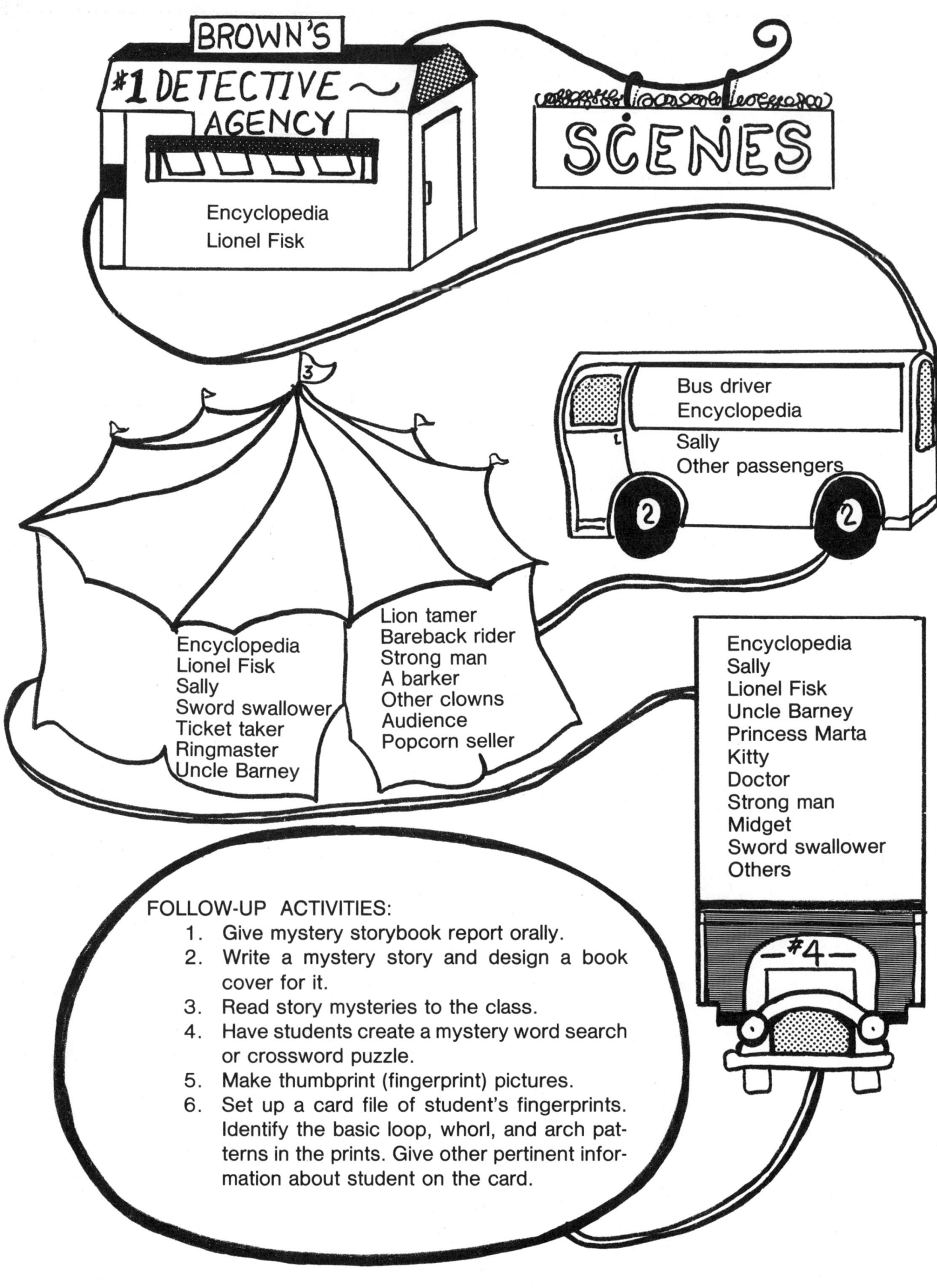

BROWN'S #1 DETECTIVE ~ AGENCY

Encyclopedia
Lionel Fisk

SCENES

Bus driver
Encyclopedia
Sally
Other passengers

Encyclopedia
Lionel Fisk
Sally
Sword swallower
Ticket taker
Ringmaster
Uncle Barney

Lion tamer
Bareback rider
Strong man
A barker
Other clowns
Audience
Popcorn seller

Encyclopedia
Sally
Lionel Fisk
Uncle Barney
Princess Marta
Kitty
Doctor
Strong man
Midget
Sword swallower
Others

#4

FOLLOW-UP ACTIVITIES:
1. Give mystery storybook report orally.
2. Write a mystery story and design a book cover for it.
3. Read story mysteries to the class.
4. Have students create a mystery word search or crossword puzzle.
5. Make thumbprint (fingerprint) pictures.
6. Set up a card file of student's fingerprints. Identify the basic loop, whorl, and arch patterns in the prints. Give other pertinent information about student on the card.

SUPER SLEUTH'S REPORT

Sleuth's Name _____

Address _____

_____

| Thumbprint |

Height _____   Weight _____   Age _____

Title of Mystery _____

Author _____

    A super sleuth must accurately report the facts to help solve the mystery. Give accurate, detailed information for each of these mystery story elements.

Clues Found in the Story

Mystery or Crime

Excitement in the Story

Method of Detection Used

Suspense in the Story

A ttention M ysteries Y ield S uspenseful T errific & E xciting R eading for Y ou

WRITE A MYSTERY STORY...

Be a detective and devise your plan of action...

I. What is the mystery or crime?

II. Who committed the crime?

III. Why was the crime committed?

IV. How was it committed?

V. Who are some of the other characters involved (who solves the mystery, is there a partner or friend, are there any witnesses, etc.)?

VI. Give the setting of the mystery (time and place).

A mystery story needs a beginning (the introduction of the setting and some of the characters), a development (telling about the events, clues, the climax), and a resolution (an ending) to be complete.

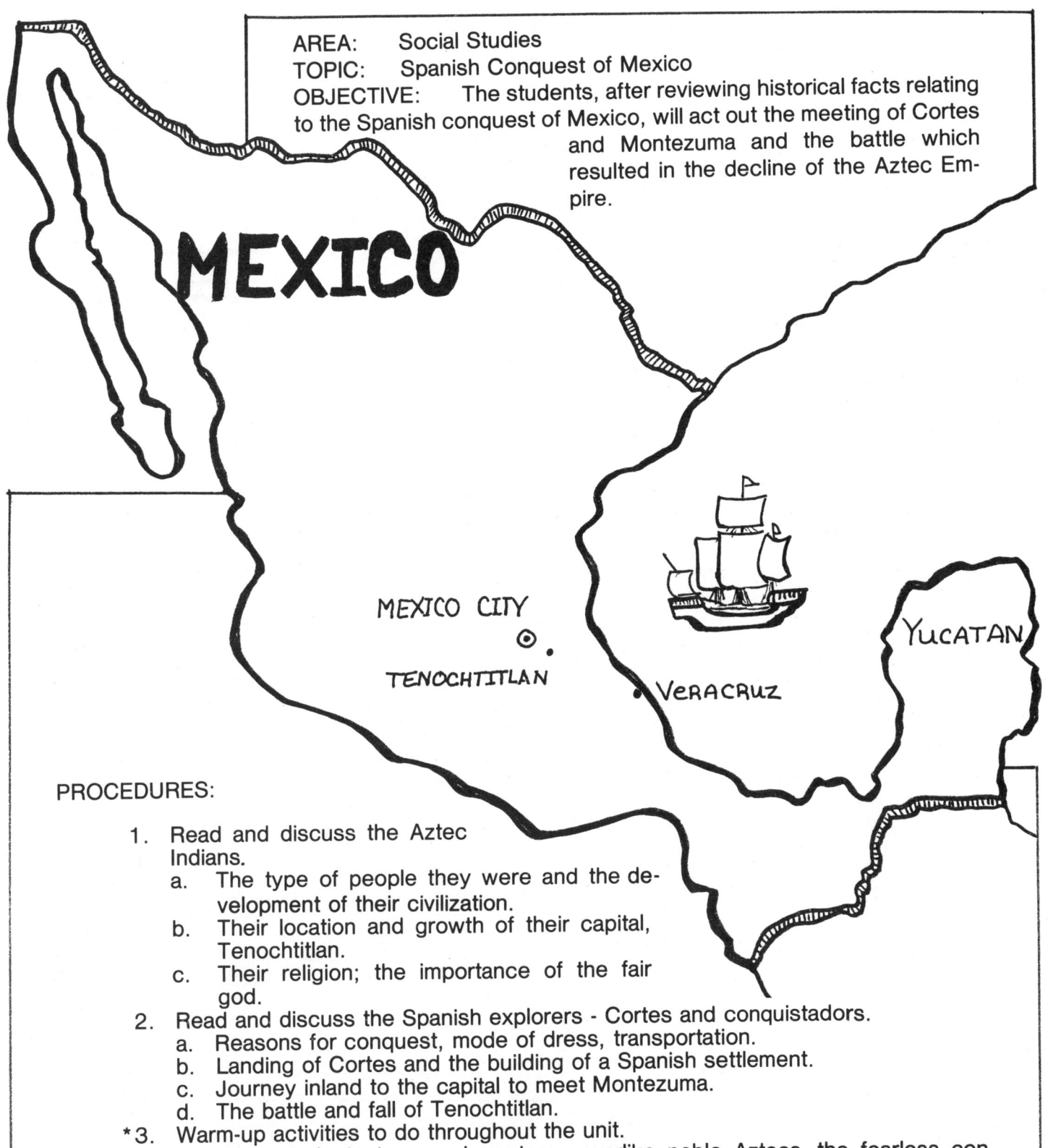

AREA: Social Studies
TOPIC: Spanish Conquest of Mexico
OBJECTIVE: The students, after reviewing historical facts relating to the Spanish conquest of Mexico, will act out the meeting of Cortes and Montezuma and the battle which resulted in the decline of the Aztec Empire.

MEXICO

MEXICO CITY
⊙ .
TENOCHTITLAN

. VERACRUZ

YUCATAN

PROCEDURES:

1. Read and discuss the Aztec Indians.
   a. The type of people they were and the development of their civilization.
   b. Their location and growth of their capital, Tenochtitlan.
   c. Their religion; the importance of the fair god.
2. Read and discuss the Spanish explorers - Cortes and conquistadors.
   a. Reasons for conquest, mode of dress, transportation.
   b. Landing of Cortes and the building of a Spanish settlement.
   c. Journey inland to the capital to meet Montezuma.
   d. The battle and fall of Tenochtitlan.
*3. Warm-up activities to do throughout the unit.
   a. Have students try on characters - warlike noble Aztecs, the fearless conquistadors, leaders Cortes and Montezuma.
   b. Side Coaching: the type of character expressions and movements students should portray.
*4. Role play mini-situations to help students develop a feel for the characters and situations.
   a. Aztecs conquering other tribes.
   b. A religious ceremony of the Aztecs.
   c. Cortes' landing with his ships - building of their settlement.
   d. Cortes' journeying inland to the capital.

5. Discuss the meeting of Cortes and Montezuma and the resulting battles. Have students sequence the events on the board.

6. Set the scenes: In the room set the location of the city: Montezuma's palace, the entrance of Cortes and the route to follow to the city. This should require minimal movement of furniture.

7. The teacher can decide whether to involve all students or to use only half the class while the rest play the audience.

*8. The teacher narrates the sequenced events while the students pantomime the actions. After going through the events once, sit down and discuss what you liked - changes or additions to be made, verbal conversations to be added in addition to narration. Students might change roles.

*9. Rerun the pantomime with changes as the teacher narrates.

10. Complete the time line activity.

11. Divide the class into small groups. Assign an event to each group. Have the group illustrate that event. Use each illustration to make a class time line.

TIME LINE

Fill in the appropriate events in the correct sequential order. Illustrate the mode of dress of a conquistador and an Aztec.

AN UNEASY PEACE

FALL OF TENOCHTITLAN

BURNING OF THE VESSELS

INITIAL MEETING OF AZTECS

REBUILDING OF THE CAPITAL CITY

MARCHING THROUGH THE JUNGLE

SLAUGHTER OF THE AZTEC PEOPLE

LANDING AND UNLOADING OF BOATS

ESTABLISHING SPANISH SETTLEMENTS

1521

1519

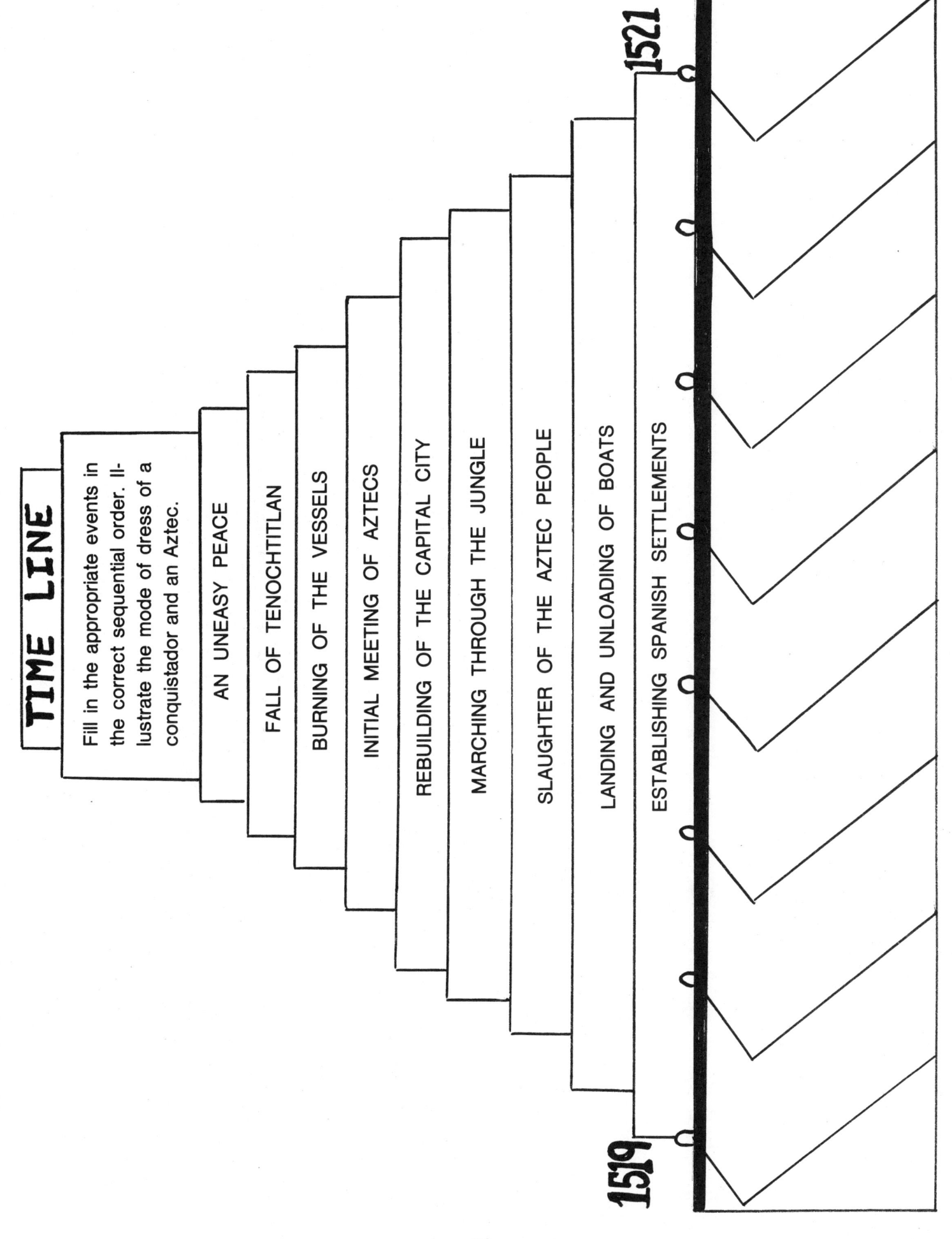

AREA: Social Studies

TOPIC: Pilgrims

OBJECTIVE: To become aware of and increase the students' knowledge of the Pilgrims.

PROCEDURE:

1. Discuss with the students the idea of moving to a new town - why a move might take place and the emotions of various family members.

2. As a class have the children list things their family would take if they had to move.

3. Discuss and give information about the Pilgrims' journey.

4. As a class make a list of the things the Pilgrims were allowed to take - for example, swords, guns, tools, cooking utensils, one chest for clothing, Bible.

5. Compare and contrast the Pilgrims' list to the students' list. At this point, through their discussions, the children will realize that if they were Pilgrim children they would not have been allowed to take their toys, pets and other prized possessions.

*6. Have each child think of his favorite possession. Choose students to take the role of father, mother and child.
    Role play the situation of a Pilgrim child trying to convince her parents to allow her to take that possession with them to America. Replay this situation 2 or 3 times choosing new players.

7. Have each child write about "The Things I Left Behind." (See Activity Sheet.)

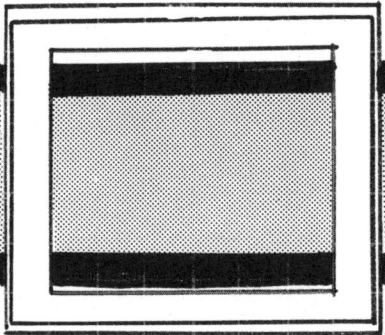

FOLLOW-UP ACTIVITIES:

1. Illustrate their stories.

2. Write about the Pilgrims' journey.

3. Draw pictures of the Mayflower.

4. Re-enact the Pilgrim/Indian feast.

"THE THINGS I LEFT BEHIND!"

AREA: Social Studies
TOPIC: Feelings
OBJECTIVE: To become aware of and be able to express feelings through body movement.

PROCEDURE:

1. Discuss feelings and emotions and what might cause them. Using their faces and arms, have the students show you - happy, angry, sad, surprised, frightened.

*2. Find a self-space in the room. Ask students to walk like:

an old man with a cane
a stranger in a dark, deserted park
a very short person in huge snowdrifts
a boy walking down the street who just found $5.00
a frightened girl on a lonely street
an angry boy getting ready to fight

NOTE: A good way to get the children to move freely is to use music that might evoke the feelings of happy, sad, frightened, etc.

*3. Act out situations that would show various emotions. Examples:

Conflict between family members at the dinner table.
Waiting to find out if you got a lead in the school play.
An argument over a football game.
You just found out that your pet has died.
Baby-sitting in a strange house with unfamiliar sounds coming from the basement.

4. Write about an experience when there was great emotion shown.

Next to each picture write about a time you felt the way each face looks.

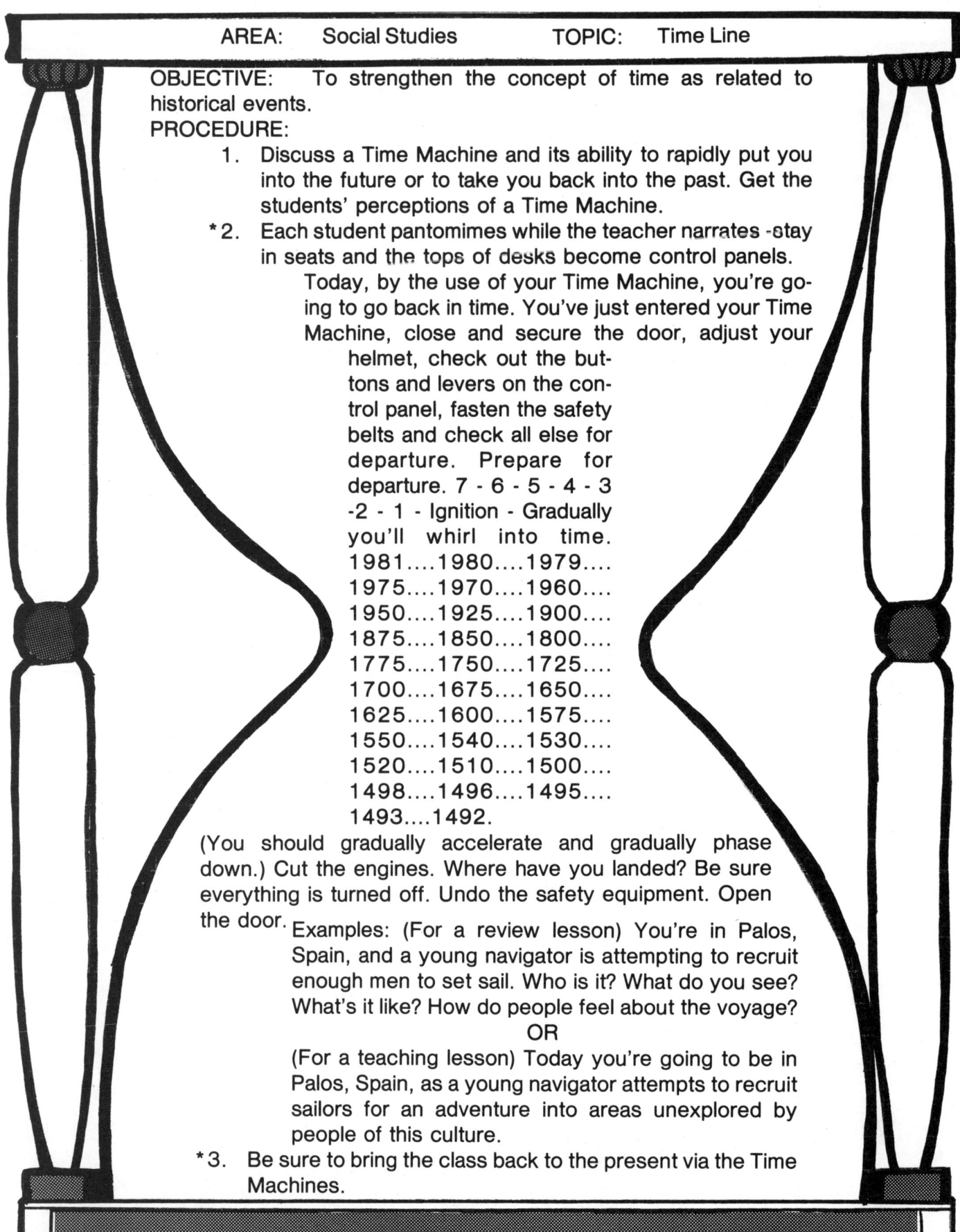

AREA: Social Studies   TOPIC: Time Line

OBJECTIVE: To strengthen the concept of time as related to historical events.

PROCEDURE:

1. Discuss a Time Machine and its ability to rapidly put you into the future or to take you back into the past. Get the students' perceptions of a Time Machine.

*2. Each student pantomimes while the teacher narrates -stay in seats and the tops of desks become control panels.

Today, by the use of your Time Machine, you're going to go back in time. You've just entered your Time Machine, close and secure the door, adjust your helmet, check out the buttons and levers on the control panel, fasten the safety belts and check all else for departure. Prepare for departure. 7 - 6 - 5 - 4 - 3 -2 - 1 - Ignition - Gradually you'll whirl into time. 1981....1980....1979.... 1975....1970....1960.... 1950....1925....1900.... 1875....1850....1800.... 1775....1750....1725.... 1700....1675....1650.... 1625....1600....1575.... 1550....1540....1530.... 1520....1510....1500.... 1498....1496....1495.... 1493....1492.

(You should gradually accelerate and gradually phase down.) Cut the engines. Where have you landed? Be sure everything is turned off. Undo the safety equipment. Open the door.

Examples: (For a review lesson) You're in Palos, Spain, and a young navigator is attempting to recruit enough men to set sail. Who is it? What do you see? What's it like? How do people feel about the voyage?

OR

(For a teaching lesson) Today you're going to be in Palos, Spain, as a young navigator attempts to recruit sailors for an adventure into areas unexplored by people of this culture.

*3. Be sure to bring the class back to the present via the Time Machines.

AREA: Social Studies
TOPIC: Occupations
OBJECTIVE: An awareness of various occupations and their required skills.

PROCEDURE:
1. Elicit numerous occupations from the students. List them on the board.

TEACHER DOCTOR MECHANIC CLERK SECRETARY
NURSE CASHIER PILOT BAKER CARPENTER BALL PLAYER
BARBER LAWYER POLICE TRUCKER BEAUTICIAN FIREMAN FARMER
LABORER

2. Discuss what qualities a person has to have in order to perform the job. Examples:

Policeman - Strong, intelligent, patient, organized

Secretary - Ability to type well, pleasant, organized

Teacher - Like children, intelligent, patient, organized

*3. Discuss an occupation and the various activities involved in it. Example:

Teacher -

Writes on the board

Teaches large and small groups

Meets with individual students

Checks papers

Organizes the room

Prepares materials

Uses A.V. equipment

Takes class on field trips

Choose students to pantomime several of the above activities for the class. Repeat this procedure with other occupations.

*4. Use the Oh-up, Oh-down technique and pantomime various situations that might occur in several occupations.

Oh-up, Oh-down. Come up as a fireman at a huge house fire. Get the hose, pull it out, turn it on and start to spray. Look, there's someone upstairs. Get the ladder and climb up. Oh-up, Oh-down. Come up as a bank teller. Someone's come to cash a check. Look it over, ask for identification. Write down his driver's license number. Get the money and count it out. Oh-up, Oh-down, etc.

5. Discussion:

Is it important to be able to choose what you do for a living? Why?

Could you ever change your mind?

What reasons would there be for someone to change his mind?

Does the job you choose dictate where you'll live?

6. Write about and illustrate the topic "When I Grow Up."
(See Activity Page.)

FOLLOW-UP ACTIVITIES:
1. Invite speakers to class.
2. Research prerequisites for occupations.
*3. Pantomime their chosen occupation.
*4. Group pantomime showing interactions between occupations.

WHEN I GROW UP.....

ME MOBILE

AREA: Social Studies
TOPIC: Self-Awareness
OBJECTIVE: To develop a greater awareness of yourself by sharing information and feelings with others.

PROCEDURE:
1. Discuss the ways you become acquainted with a person, for example, by knowing about his interests, likes, dislikes, his past, hopes for the future, feelings.

*2. In groups, students pantomime something revealing about themselves to help others become better acquainted with them (likes, dislikes, interests, hobbies, favorites, etc.).
   a. Divide the class into groups of 7 or 8.
   b. Seat the groups in their given areas.
   c. All groups are operating simultaneously:
      1) Groups mutually agree on who starts within their group.
      2) They take turns miming while the rest of their group guesses what they're sharing about themselves.
      3) Stress cooperation.
      4) May have a second turn within their group after everyone has had an opportunity to share.
      5) May do the same as someone else if it applies to themselves.

3. Discussion following mimes:
   What can you say about the things you learned about each other?
   What similarities did you notice about the hobbies, interests, likes, dislikes?
   What differences did you notice about the hobbies, interests, likes, dislikes?
   Is it acceptable to be similar?
   Is it acceptable to be different?
   Why do you feel as you do?

FOLLOW-UP ACTIVITIES:

1. Construct mobiles of important things in their lives.
2. Write acrostic poems using their names.
3. Write riddles about themselves giving ____ facts.
4. Design a coat of arms, shield, or crest about themselves.
5. Write an autobiography.
6. Sketch portraits of themselves by using a mirror. Add color.

STATISTICS

My full name is _____.

My address is _____.
(number & street)

_____
(city,   state,   zip code)

My age is _____. My birth date is _____.

My mother's name is _____.

Her occupation is _____.

My father's name is _____.

His occupation is _____.

I live with _____.

I have _____ brothers and _____ sisters.

INTERESTS

Some of my favorites are:

Book _____   Indoor game _____

Magazine _____   Outdoor game _____

Comic book _____   Food _____

Song _____   TV program _____

Singer _____   Movie _____

School subject _____   Performer _____

MISCELLANEOUS

What things do you do when you have spare time?

If you had $1,500, what would you do with it?

AREA: Language Arts

TOPIC: Haiku

OBJECTIVE: To increase appreciation of poetry and to write a poem.

PROCEDURE:

1. Brainstorm with the class and list on the board descriptive words and phrases about TREES - for example, budding, blossoming, barren, leafy, needles, falling leaves, leaves changing colors, gnarled, craggy, smooth bark, nuts, fruits, provides homes for birds and squirrels, gets glazed by sleet and weighted down by snow, twisting and whipping around in the wind, etc.

*2. Oh-up, Oh-down technique: try becoming a tree under various circumstances. Students find a self-space:

Oh-up, Oh-down. Come up as a hardwood tree standing in the middle of an open field with three feet of snow about your trunk and your limbs laden with thick pillows of snow. A gusty wind comes up and gradually increases in strength. Then all settles into a peaceful quiet stillness. Oh-up, Oh-down. Come up as a gnarled cherry tree in the spring in an orchard. The tree develops blossoms followed by fruit. The fruit is picked by a shaking picking machine. Then barren, you stand in the winter snow. Oh-up, Oh-down. Come up as....

   a. An evergreen tree with birds flitting in and out.
   b. A stately tree in the forest, reaching toward the sun.
   c. A seed that by chance fell onto fertile soil with sufficient sunlight and space to grow.
   d. A sturdy maple tree in a backyard used for climbing.
   e. A tree caught in a forest fire that had been started by lightning.
   f. A small pine tree that provides shelter for a rabbit and a home for a bird.

3. Explain Haiku poetry and read some examples. Stress counting syllables.
4. Write a Haiku poem dealing with trees. Write another Haiku poem about another aspect of nature.

FOLLOW-UP ACTIVITIES:
   1. Illustrate with watercolors.
   2. Make a class booklet.
   3. Make a greeting card.

HAIKU POETRY

Haiku (hi′ ku) is a short Japanese poem that expresses an observation, experience, or thought about some aspect of nature. It often refers to a season, either directly or implied, through the choice of words.

Haiku is usually 17 syllables long in 3 unrhymed lines. The lines are 5 syllables, 7 syllables, and 5 syllables.

Perfect golden leaves
Fluttering in the soft breeze
Waving a good-by.

Beautiful blossoms
Such fragile softness adorns
A gnarled cherry tree.

Juniper berries
Calmly wait expectantly
A hungry bird's meal.

Busy ladybug
Rests peacefully on a leaf
Soon you'll fly away.

71

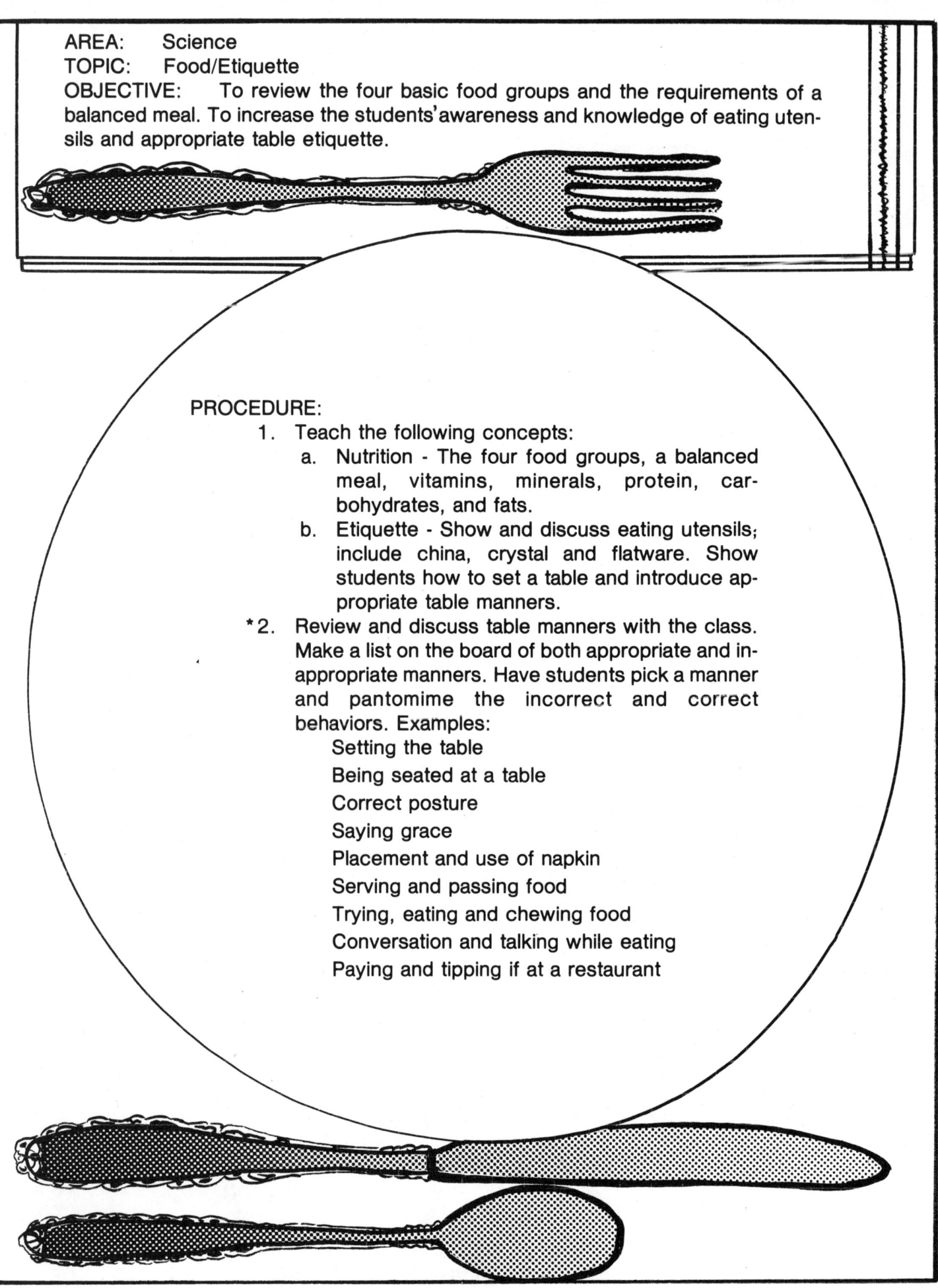

AREA: Science
TOPIC: Food/Etiquette
OBJECTIVE: To review the four basic food groups and the requirements of a balanced meal. To increase the students'awareness and knowledge of eating utensils and appropriate table etiquette.

PROCEDURE:
1. Teach the following concepts:
    a. Nutrition - The four food groups, a balanced meal, vitamins, minerals, protein, carbohydrates, and fats.
    b. Etiquette - Show and discuss eating utensils; include china, crystal and flatware. Show students how to set a table and introduce appropriate table manners.
*2. Review and discuss table manners with the class. Make a list on the board of both appropriate and inappropriate manners. Have students pick a manner and pantomime the incorrect and correct behaviors. Examples:
    Setting the table

    Being seated at a table

    Correct posture

    Saying grace

    Placement and use of napkin

    Serving and passing food

    Trying, eating and chewing food

    Conversation and talking while eating

    Paying and tipping if at a restaurant

*3. A whole group activity would be to role play a dinner situation. Each student uses his desk as a dinner table with a place setting in front of him. The teacher guides the class through dinner, giving directions for actions. Using the words freeze and unfreeze, side coaching can be used to give additional information or instruction.

4. Discuss with the class different dinner situations - formal and informal, various dinner locations, for example, home, restaurant, park, neighbor's house.

*5. Have the students form groups with 3 or 4 students per group. Each group is to create a dinner situation. They will need to assign character roles, for example, a family, a parent and children, a group of friends, a couple. Decide whether the skit will be pantomime or contain dialog. In each skit the characters need to:
  a. Set a table correctly,
  b. Have a balanced meal,
  c. Act out at least five correct table manners.
The groups need to practice and present the skits to the rest of the class.

NOTE: Students will want to make props or bring things from home. This works out well.

6. Optional - Use the activity sheet (see next page) as a group or individual report after all the skits have been presented.

FOLLOW-UP ACTIVITIES:
  1. Make a menu with balanced meals.
  2. Write about an embarrassing dinner situation.
  3. Describe your favorite meal.

NAMES OF STUDENTS IN YOUR GROUP -

SITUATION -

CHARACTER ROLES -

MENU -

CORRECT MANNERS DISPLAYED -

EVALUATION OF SKIT -

AREA: Science   TOPIC: Simple Machines

OBJECTIVE: To develop the concept of a simple machine and to identify nine simple machines.

PROCEDURE:
1. Teach the concepts.
   a. Definition of work
   b. Types of energy we use
   c. Operation of tools - define load and effort
   d. Three types of machines - simple, compound, complex
   e. Importance of machines to man

2. Review the definitions of a simple machine. Stress the number of moving parts.

3. Introduce nine simple machines -
   Pulley   Lever/Fulcrum   Wedge
   Wheel and Axle Chisel   Inclined Plane
   Hinge   Gear   Screw (winding inclined plane)

Have the class identify each machine by using pictures, tools from home or objects in the room. Discuss their operation, importance and uses.

*4. Divide the class into groups containing 3 or 4 students. The group must select at least 3 simple machines listed above that they can form by using their bodies and body movements. Examples:

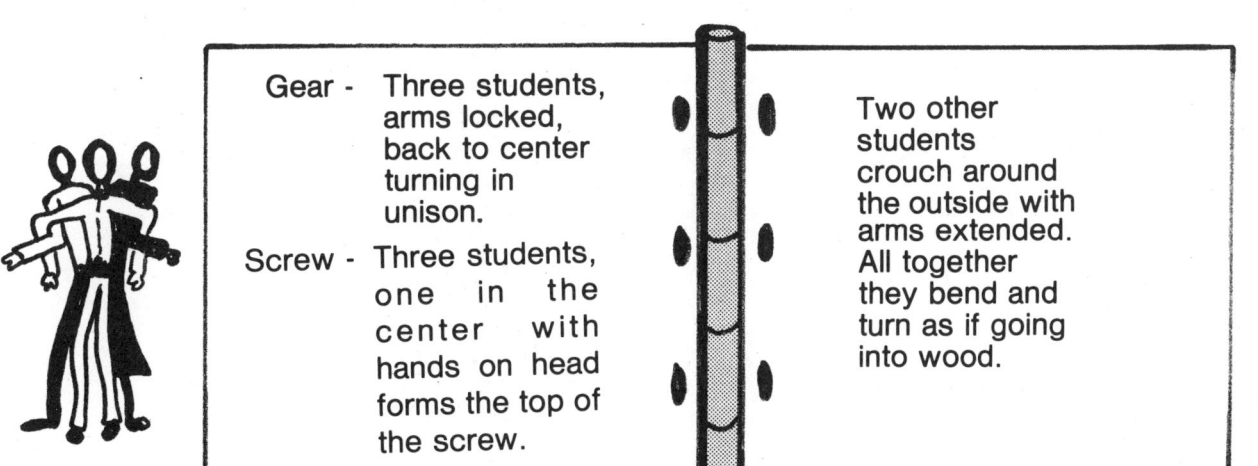

Gear - Three students, arms locked, back to center turning in unison.

Screw - Three students, one in the center with hands on head forms the top of the screw. Two other students crouch around the outside with arms extended. All together they bend and turn as if going into wood.

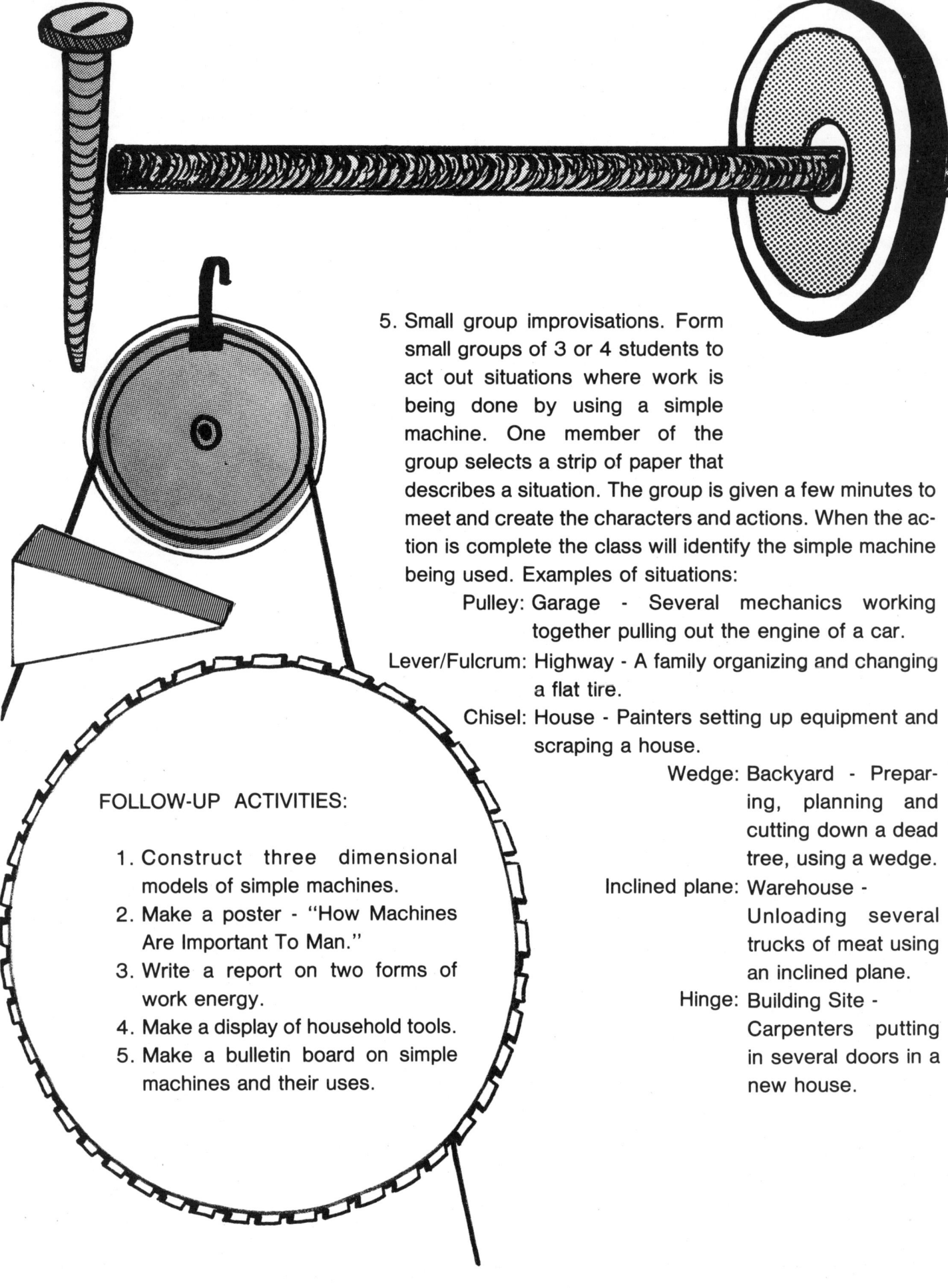

5. Small group improvisations. Form small groups of 3 or 4 students to act out situations where work is being done by using a simple machine. One member of the group selects a strip of paper that describes a situation. The group is given a few minutes to meet and create the characters and actions. When the action is complete the class will identify the simple machine being used. Examples of situations:

Pulley: Garage - Several mechanics working together pulling out the engine of a car.

Lever/Fulcrum: Highway - A family organizing and changing a flat tire.

Chisel: House - Painters setting up equipment and scraping a house.

Wedge: Backyard - Preparing, planning and cutting down a dead tree, using a wedge.

Inclined plane: Warehouse - Unloading several trucks of meat using an inclined plane.

Hinge: Building Site - Carpenters putting in several doors in a new house.

FOLLOW-UP ACTIVITIES:

1. Construct three dimensional models of simple machines.
2. Make a poster - "How Machines Are Important To Man."
3. Write a report on two forms of work energy.
4. Make a display of household tools.
5. Make a bulletin board on simple machines and their uses.

Draw an illustration of each machine and give one way it is used.

Define Simple Machine -

HINGE: USE:	SCREW: USE:	WEDGE: USE:
PULLEY: USE:	WHEEL/AXLE: USE:	LEVER/FULCRUM: USE:
GEAR: USE:	CHISEL: USE:	INCLINED PLANE: USE:

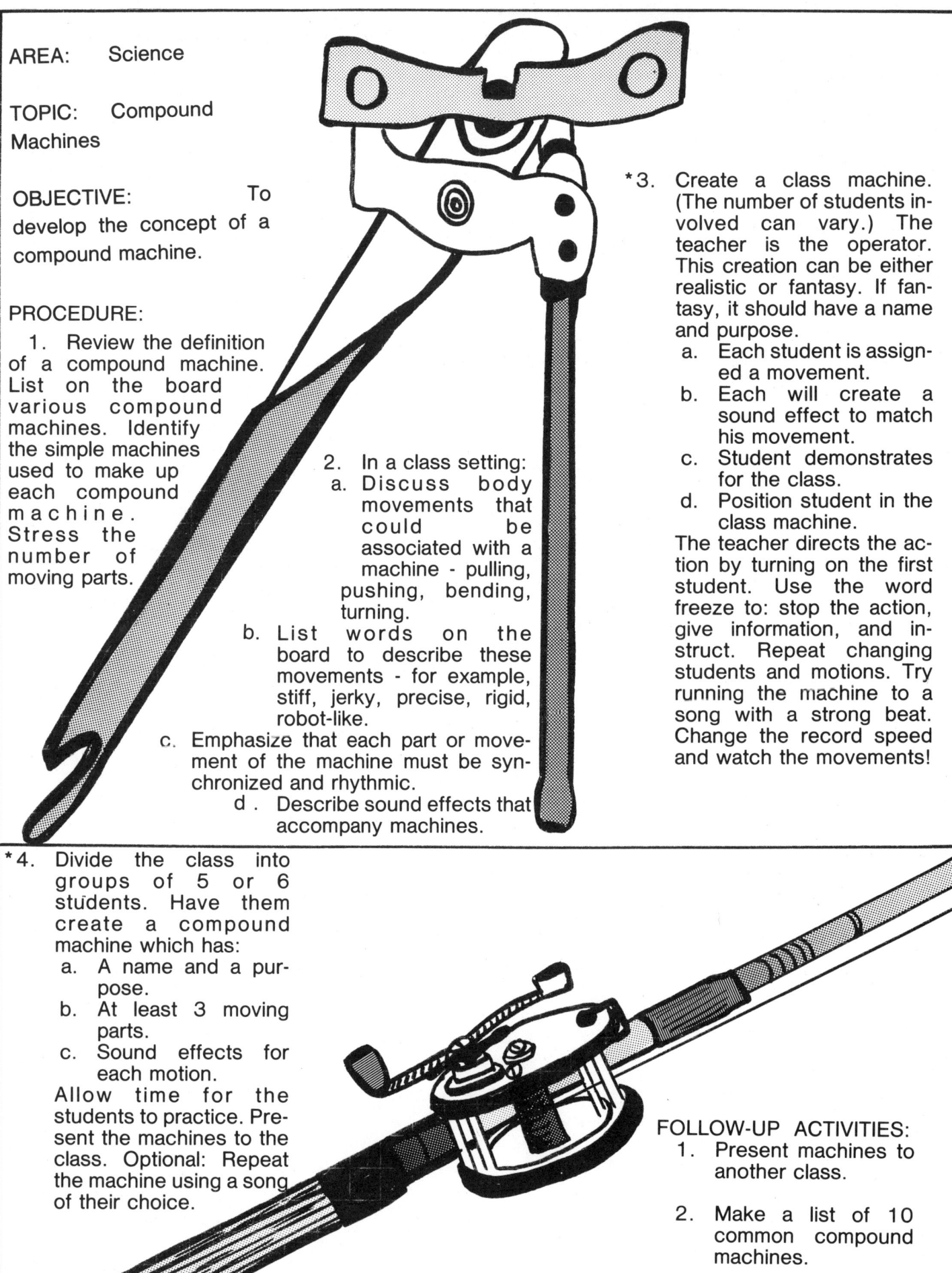

AREA: Science

TOPIC: Compound Machines

OBJECTIVE: To develop the concept of a compound machine.

PROCEDURE:

1. Review the definition of a compound machine. List on the board various compound machines. Identify the simple machines used to make up each compound machine. Stress the number of moving parts.

2. In a class setting:
a. Discuss body movements that could be associated with a machine - pulling, pushing, bending, turning.
b. List words on the board to describe these movements - for example, stiff, jerky, precise, rigid, robot-like.
c. Emphasize that each part or movement of the machine must be synchronized and rhythmic.
d. Describe sound effects that accompany machines.

*3. Create a class machine. (The number of students involved can vary.) The teacher is the operator. This creation can be either realistic or fantasy. If fantasy, it should have a name and purpose.
a. Each student is assigned a movement.
b. Each will create a sound effect to match his movement.
c. Student demonstrates for the class.
d. Position student in the class machine.
The teacher directs the action by turning on the first student. Use the word freeze to: stop the action, give information, and instruct. Repeat changing students and motions. Try running the machine to a song with a strong beat. Change the record speed and watch the movements!

*4. Divide the class into groups of 5 or 6 students. Have them create a compound machine which has:
a. A name and a purpose.
b. At least 3 moving parts.
c. Sound effects for each motion.
Allow time for the students to practice. Present the machines to the class. Optional: Repeat the machine using a song of their choice.

FOLLOW-UP ACTIVITIES:
1. Present machines to another class.

2. Make a list of 10 common compound machines.

AREA: Math/Reading
TOPIC: Measurement/Categorization
OBJECTIVE: To measure accurately and follow a recipe. To accurately categorize items.

PROCEDURE:

1. Class Project - Make ice cream - Have everyone make his own serving by using a metal can, plastic bowl, and a tongue depressor. IT'S GREAT! (See recipe on the next page.)

2. Elicit action words involved in making ice cream. List these on the board (shopping, measuring, talking, mixing, stirring, washing, deciding, paying, carrying, checking, tasting, giggling, smiling, drying, mopping, etc.).

3. Each student will categorize the action words listed on the board according to when they were used in the ice-cream making process. (Use the Activity Sheet provided.)

*4. Do short pantomimes of some of the action words listed on the board in a self-space (measuring, mixing, tasting).

OR

Narrate a Chain Pantomime of part of the process of making the ice cream.
Shopping: Drive to the store, get out of the car, enter the store, get a shopping cart, push it down the aisles, pick up the ingredients one at a time (some on top shelves/others lower), change minds after checking quantities and prices of brands, put items in the cart (some are heavy/others light), check out, pay, leave store, put groceries into the car, get in yourself.

5. Give positive feedback on specific actions you observed being done well.

FOLLOW-UP ACTIVITIES:
1. Write and illustrate an experience with ice cream.
2. Investigate the history of ice cream.
3. Research why salt melts ice.
4. Make an hypothesis about which ice cream flavors are the top sellers. Check it out at several local ice-cream stores.

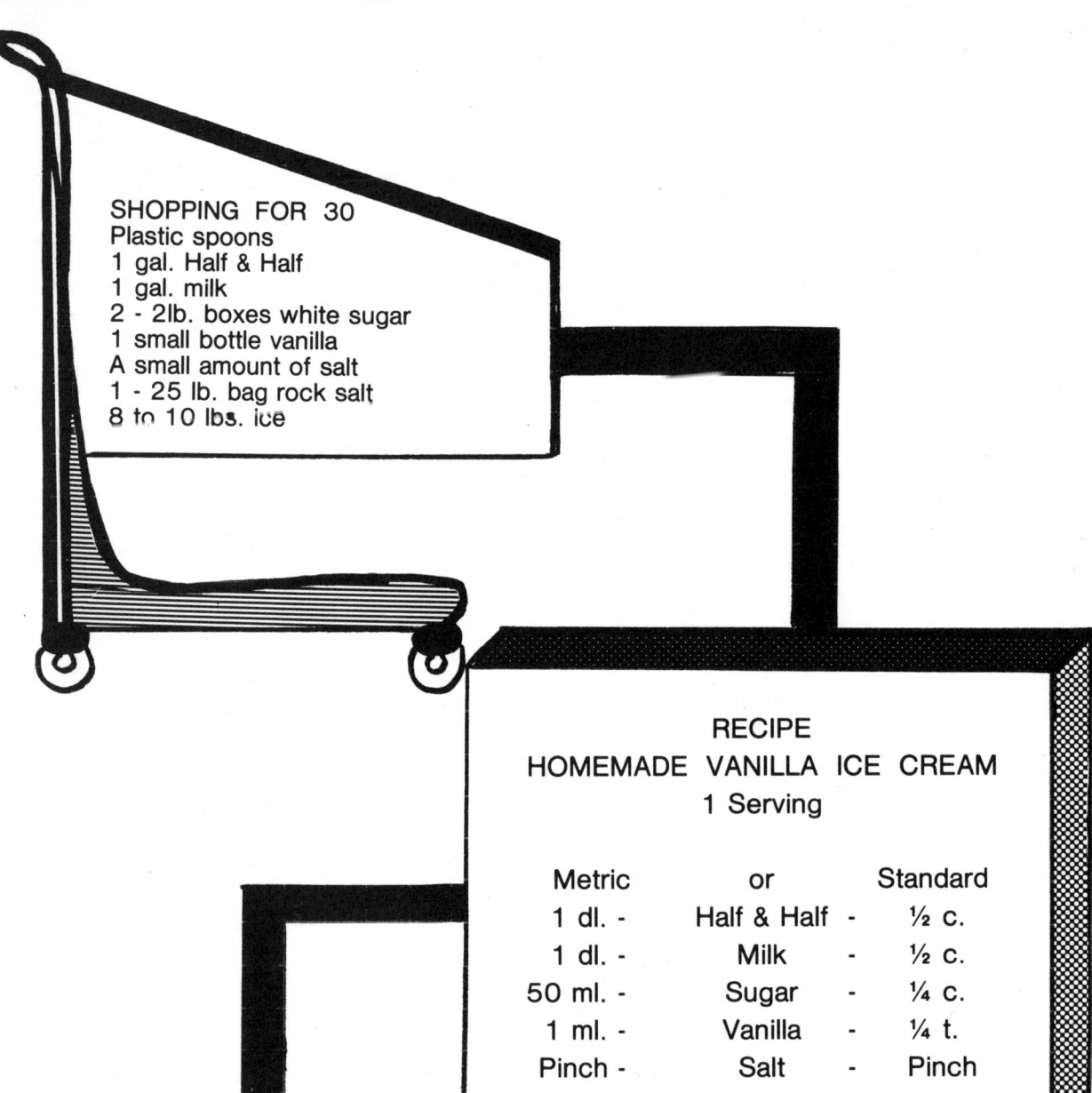

SHOPPING FOR 30
Plastic spoons
1 gal. Half & Half
1 gal. milk
2 - 2lb. boxes white sugar
1 small bottle vanilla
A small amount of salt
1 - 25 lb. bag rock salt
8 to 10 lbs. ice

RECIPE
HOMEMADE VANILLA ICE CREAM
1 Serving

Metric	or		Standard
1 dl. -	Half & Half	-	½ c.
1 dl. -	Milk	-	½ c.
50 ml. -	Sugar	-	¼ c.
1 ml. -	Vanilla	-	¼ t.
Pinch -	Salt	-	Pinch

Step by Step:
1. Put ingredients in can and mix well.
2. Cover the can with paper and set in the bowl.
3. Put alternate layers of ice and rock salt around the can. Be generous with the salt.
4. Uncover the can and wait.
5. Stir when it starts to harden on the inside edge of can. Continue to stir slowly.
6. Add ice and salt as needed. Drain off excess water when necessary.
7. When mixture is thick, drain off water and repack ice and salt around the can using much more salt.
8. Cover with newspaper; let it set so flavor can spread and hardening can take place.
9. Eat!
10. Clean up…

MAKING ICE CREAM

Directions: Write the action words listed on the board in the correct categories. Words can be used more than one time and other action words can be added.

I. Preparation (Getting Ready)	II. Making

III. Eating	IV. Cleanup

Write about making the ice cream. Be sure to tell it in the order it happened.

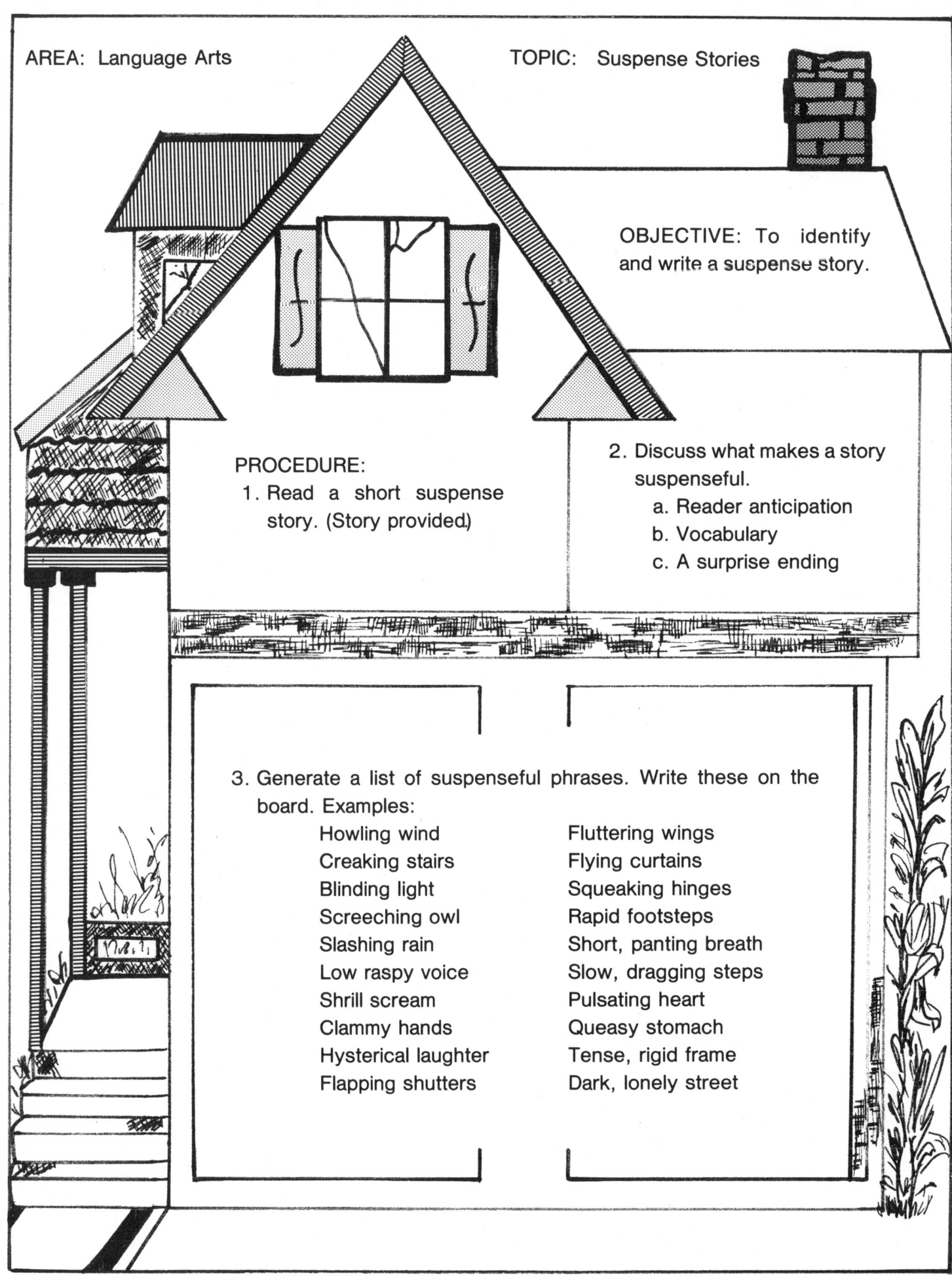

AREA: Language Arts

TOPIC: Suspense Stories

OBJECTIVE: To identify and write a suspense story.

PROCEDURE:

1. Read a short suspense story. (Story provided)

2. Discuss what makes a story suspenseful.
   a. Reader anticipation
   b. Vocabulary
   c. A surprise ending

3. Generate a list of suspenseful phrases. Write these on the board. Examples:

Howling wind	Fluttering wings
Creaking stairs	Flying curtains
Blinding light	Squeaking hinges
Screeching owl	Rapid footsteps
Slashing rain	Short, panting breath
Low raspy voice	Slow, dragging steps
Shrill scream	Pulsating heart
Clammy hands	Queasy stomach
Hysterical laughter	Tense, rigid frame
Flapping shutters	Dark, lonely street

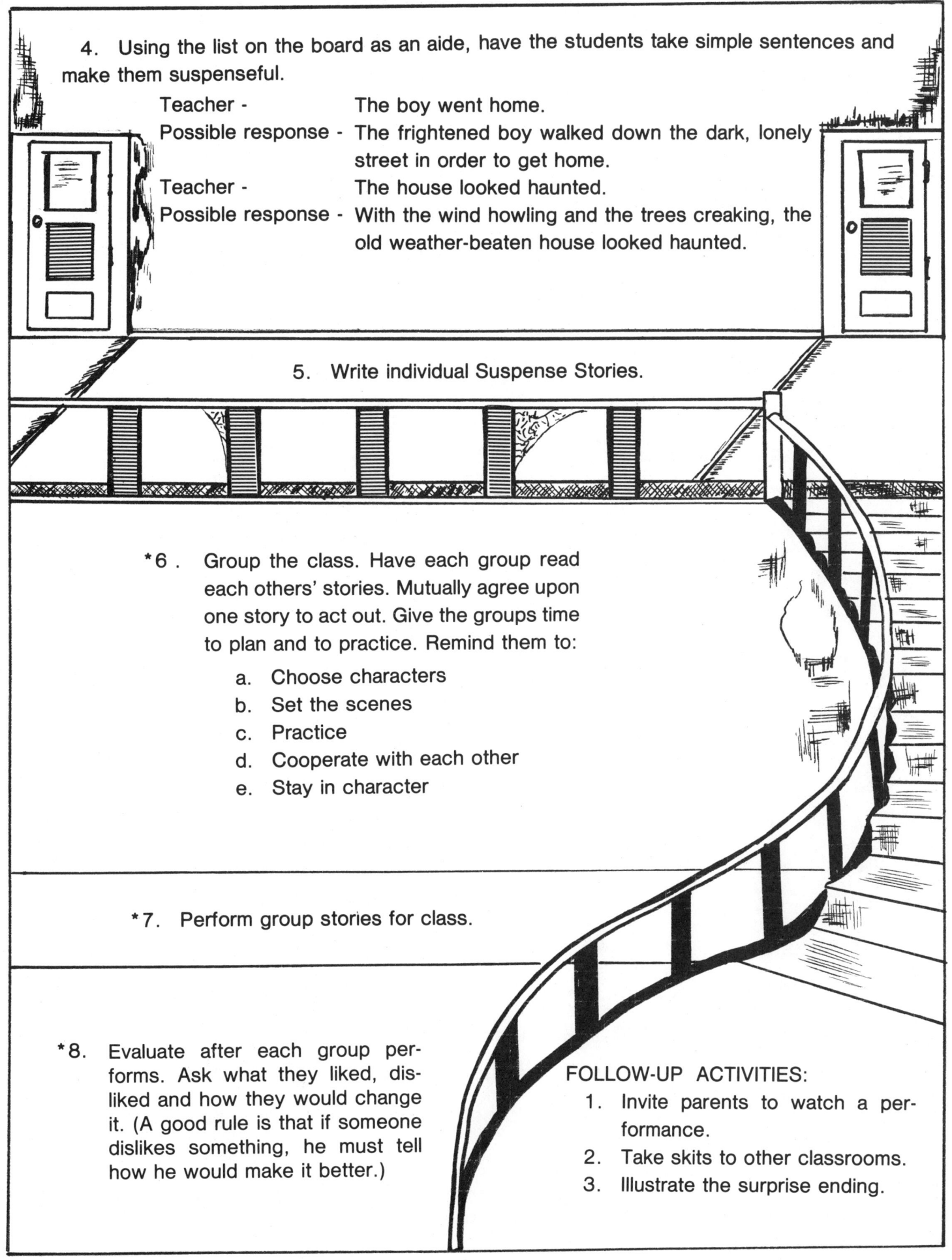

4. Using the list on the board as an aide, have the students take simple sentences and make them suspenseful.

        Teacher -   The boy went home.
        Possible response -   The frightened boy walked down the dark, lonely street in order to get home.
        Teacher -   The house looked haunted.
        Possible response -   With the wind howling and the trees creaking, the old weather-beaten house looked haunted.

5. Write individual Suspense Stories.

*6. Group the class. Have each group read each others' stories. Mutually agree upon one story to act out. Give the groups time to plan and to practice. Remind them to:

    a. Choose characters
    b. Set the scenes
    c. Practice
    d. Cooperate with each other
    e. Stay in character

*7. Perform group stories for class.

*8. Evaluate after each group performs. Ask what they liked, disliked and how they would change it. (A good rule is that if someone dislikes something, he must tell how he would make it better.)

FOLLOW-UP ACTIVITIES:
1. Invite parents to watch a performance.
2. Take skits to other classrooms.
3. Illustrate the surprise ending.

A REALTOR'S NIGHTMARE

Shortly after I received my Real Estate license and I was in the process of opening my own office, a call came in. I was offered my first listing. The call was unusual because the house they wanted to list had been vacant for numerous years and it was known in the Real Estate trade as a "lemon." Needing the business, I agreed to go and appraise it.

I spoke to several of my friends about it and one of my close friends, who was extremely curious, asked if he could accompany me. We agreed to meet at the house the following Saturday at 6:00 p.m.

On the way over to the house, the sky darkened and it looked like we were in for some thunderstorms. Not knowing if the house had electricity, I took the flashlight. As I stood in the yard waiting for my friend, it became extremely dark and started to pour. I had to go in without him.

As I headed for the front porch I could see why the house was referred to as a lemon. It was badly weather-beaten. The paint had peeled, the shingles were falling off, and the shrubbery was terribly overgrown.

When I opened the door I was greeted with an enormous cobweb. While reaching for the lights, I thought there would have to be a lot of work done before this house would be marketable. After turning on the lights and only getting a glimpse of the inside, there was a brilliant streak of lightning followed by a sudden clap of thunder. The lights went out. I turned on the flashlight and went on in. The beam of light first stopped on a broken-down chair draped in a dusty torn sheet. As I moved the light slowly around the room, I spotted what appeared to be someone's coat bunched up in the corner, and on the floor in the middle of the room was a lone candle stub.

Just then I became aware of the sounds I hadn't noticed in my rush to turn on the lights and survey the premises. There was a scratching and scraping to my right, a soft scurrying coming through the archway that led to the next room, and overhead there seemed to be a beckoning whisper that started to draw me in the direction of the old circular stairs. I was sure it was my imagination, but as I got closer to the stairs the soft whispering seemed to be calling my name F..F..R..R..A..A..N..N..K..K....

I started up the stairs, feeling a need to check it out before I finished looking over the first floor. Again I heard the whispering; it seemed louder F..F..R..R..A..A..N..N..K..K. My mind told me this wasn't possible; it was only my nerves. However, my stomach had begun to tighten and the palms of my hands were wet. With my heart racing, I continued up the stairs with only my flashlight to show me the way. Not having been there before, I was uncertain of what lay ahead.

By this time the sky was pitch black, the thunder was rolling, the wind howled and the shutters were banging against the house. The stairwell creaked loudly and it seemed unsteady with each upward step. Suddenly, something brushed against my foot, but when I shone the light down, nothing was there. Then something seemed to rush by my head - again nothing. By the time I reached the top, I wasn't so sure I could go on. Barely a whisper above the storm I heard it again F..F..R..R..A..N..N..K..K. I summoned up all the courage I had left and turned down the hallway. The hallway was lined with several doors. The whispering had to be coming from one of them. With a swift movement I swung open one of the doors. Nothing was there. I moved down the hall and cautiously opened the next door. Before I could shine my light around that room, the lightning streaked and there was a loud CRASH. I quickly closed the door.

By now I'd had enough and decided the sale wasn't worth all of this. As I turned around to leave, I again heard the whispering. I couldn't let it go. I had to check it out. With my heart pulsating, I slowly crept to the final door. Before I could turn the knob....the door s-l-o-w-l-y swung open...I heard loud hysterical laughter....and many voices shouted "HAPPY BIRTHDAY, FRANK!"

AREA: Language Arts

TOPIC: Quotation Marks

OBJECTIVE: To correctly use quotation marks in written work.

PROCEDURE:
1. This lesson is for use after teaching usage of quotation marks. (Cartoon Strip Activity Sheet can be used as additional practice material. Have the student name the characters and rewrite in paragraph form on manuscript paper.)

*2. Role Play: Do in short time blocks and only one/two at a time.
   a. Prepare: Set up a container with slips of paper designating two characters and a topic. (See next page.)
   b. Two student volunteers choose a slip of paper and prepare to spontaneously role play the given characters and situation.
   c. While the two students role play, the rest of the class will listen carefully and write the conversation on paper using correct paragraphing, capitalization, and punctuation.

Suggestions -
   1) Inform class of who is being role played and the topic.
   2) Exchanges should be kept short.
   3) Speak slowly, loudly and clearly.

Father and son	Discuss a bike.
Mother and daughter	Discuss a hairdo.
Two students	Discuss football.
Two teenagers	Discuss a favorite record.
Mother and Father	Discuss an upcoming vacation.
Brother and sister	Discuss household chores.
Girl and salesperson	Discuss the fragrance of a perfume.
Doctor and patient	Discuss an injury.
Little kid and baby sitter	Discuss staying up longer.
Policeman and a driver	Discuss an improper turn.
Teacher and student	Discuss a recent assignment.

Rewrite in paragraph form naming the characters and telling how the words are spoken. Be sure to use indention, capitalization, and all punctuation needed.

AREA: Language Arts
TOPIC: Free Verse Poetry
OBJECTIVE: To increase an appreciation of poetry and to write a poem.

PROCEDURE:
1. Discuss and list on the board the many activities students are involved in at school - for example, being with friends, doing schoolwork, making art projects, singing.

   Note - Can transfer the activities listed to slips of paper if desired.

*2. Groups role play with/without dialog.
   a. Divide class into groups of 3, 4, or 5.
   b. Each group chooses a situation.
   c. Groups plan, prepare props, and practice.
   d. Groups share their role plays with the class.
   e. Evaluate.

3. Discuss free verse poetry and read some to the class.
   a. Has no rhyme and no regular pattern of rhythm.
   b. Doesn't have to have sentences, contains thoughts and phrases.
   c. Uses interesting words, often makes use of the senses.
   d. Uses comparisons to form word pictures.
   e. Some lines begin with capital letters.
   f. Has punctuation as needed for the natural pauses.
   g. Length of lines and poems vary.

4. Write and illustrate a free verse poem relating to school activities and associations.

FOLLOW-UP ACTIVITIES:
1. Write about memorable school events.
2. Make slides to go with the poems and do a slide/poem presentation.
3. Make posters promoting school.

Arm Hang,
Very hard to do.
The Strain,
The Pain,
The Agony.

Anita Barkley
Age 12

The sorrow I felt was greater,
Than how I felt much later.
I tried and tried.
I had to stop and so I fell,
Kerplop!

Cher Cheslow
Age 12

Wainwright,
Seven Subjects,
Teachers, Adults, Students,
  Kids,
Working, Playing, Learning,
School.

Mandy Wendland
Age 12

Wainwright Elementary School

Daydreaming is like a daze.
It's like a never ending maze.
It's wondering, pondering
And thinking what to do.
The teacher knows,
Why don't you?

Chad Borst
Age 11

Schoolwork is O.K.
And can be fun.
But sometimes I Hate It,
I Hate It, I Hate It,
And then I'm done.

Michael Flanagan
Age 12

I was in the race.
As I set the pace,
I said I must
And left them in the dust.

Tony Rolon
Age 13

Schoolwork is a drag.
I sometimes take it home in a bag.
I do it with all my might,
And sometimes I get it right!

Matt Johnson
Age 12

Before the play you get really nervous,
But during the play the nervousness goes away.
Along with the fright.
When it's over your reward is the audience's applause!

Mark Stiles
Age 11

AREA: Language Arts

TOPIC: Signal Words/Sequencing

OBJECTIVE: To identify and use signal words in written material.

PROCEDURE:
Review signal words. Generate a list of signal words and write them on the board.

Using several different cartoon strips as examples, have the students identify the actions taking place. Have them sequence the actions by using first, second, next, then and finally.

Group Pantomime -

First -   Divide the class into groups of 3 or 4.

Second - Give each group a cartoon strip to read.

Next -   Sequence the actions in the cartoon with signal words.

Then -   As a group, assign character roles and practice appropriate actions.

Finally -   Present the pantomime to the class.

Note: Encourage them to add details but not to change the story line.

Have each student create his own 5-part cartoon strip. He must include 5 signal words in the copy. The cartoon must be illustrated and colored. (See Activity Sheet)

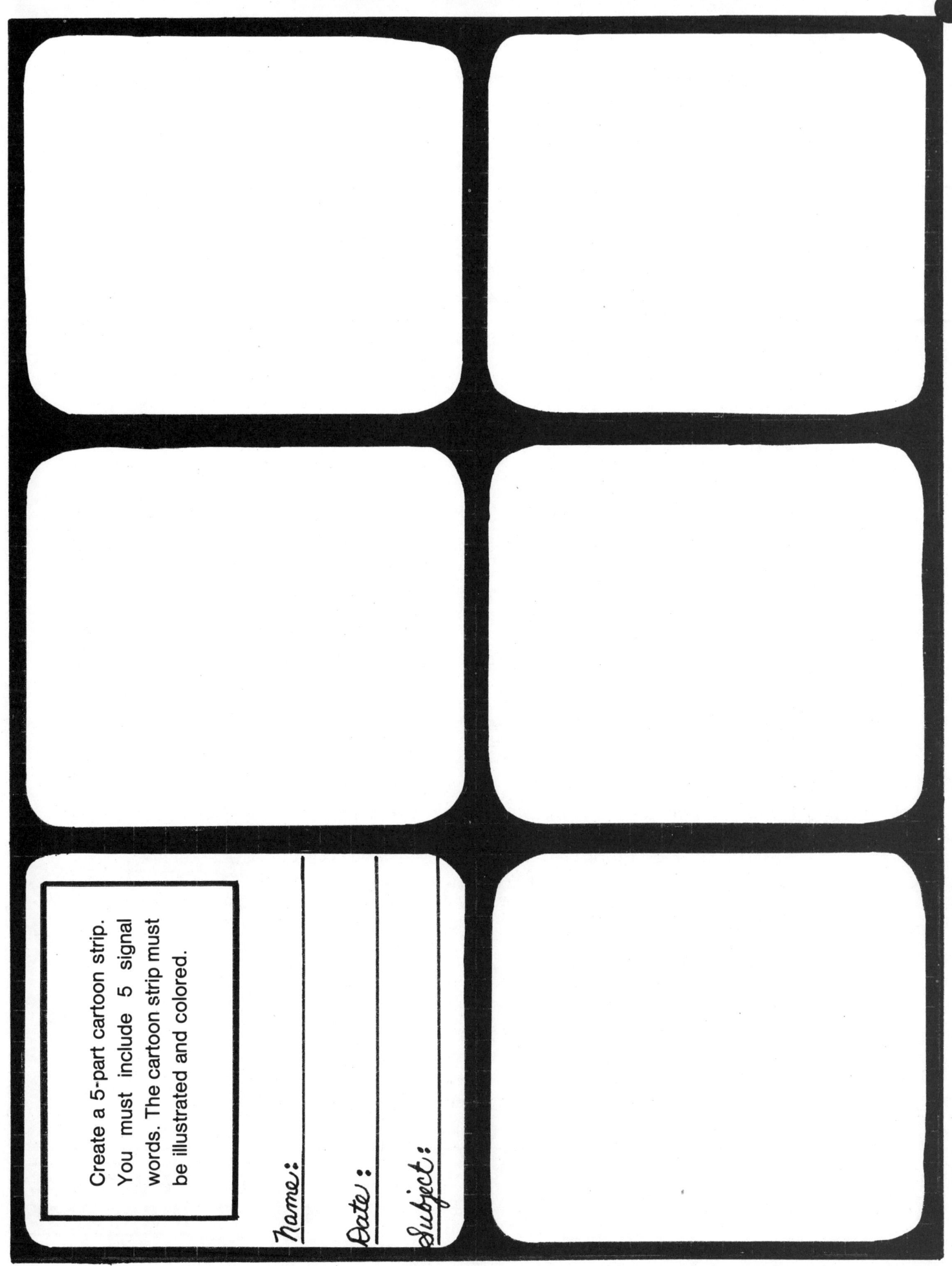

Create a 5-part cartoon strip. You must include 5 signal words. The cartoon strip must be illustrated and colored.

Name: _____

Date : _____

Subject: _____

93

START

AREA: Reading
TOPIC: Signal Words/Directions
OBJECTIVE: To identify and use signal words in direction.

PROCEDURE:
1. Discuss signal words and how they help to sequence and organize information.

2. List the words first, next, then, and finally on the board. Have the students generate a list of additional signal words - for example, after, before, second, third, while, during.

3. Using a direction, recipe, and story as examples, have the students identify the signal words in each style of writing.

*4. Act out directions in a self-space. This is a teacher-directed activity. It can be done several ways, either with an individual in front of the class, with a small group or with the whole class. Be sure the directions are simple so students can easily act them out.
   First, read a series of four directions which include signal words.
   Next, reread the directions while the students perform the required actions.
   Finally, have a student recall the signal words used.

   Possible examples to use:
   A. First, clap your hands together 4 times.
      Next clap your fingers 8 times.
      Then stamp your feet 5 times.
      Finally, slap your knees 3 times.

GO TO THE NEXT PAGE

94

B. First, stand up next to your desk.
Next do 5 knee bends.
Then, when I say go, run in place for 1 minute.
Before you quietly sit down say "Hi" to a friend.
Finally, zip your lips and give your attention to the teacher.

C. First, pick up your suitcase and walk to the elevator.
Next, push the button and wait for its arrival.
Then enter the elevator and push the button for your floor.
After the door opens, walk to your room.

D. First, put a tee in the ground and place a golf ball on it.
Next look over your clubs and select the one you want.
Then take 3 or 4 practice swings.
Finally, get set and hit a good drive.

5. Have each student write a series of five or six directions using signal words. Stress the importance of making the directions clear and simple.

*6. Divide the class into pairs and act out each other's directions. Identify the signal words used.

FOLLOW-UP ACTIVITIES:
Have students write directions -
1. From school to their house.
2. For a favorite game.
3. For a simple recipe.
4. To explain something.

STOP

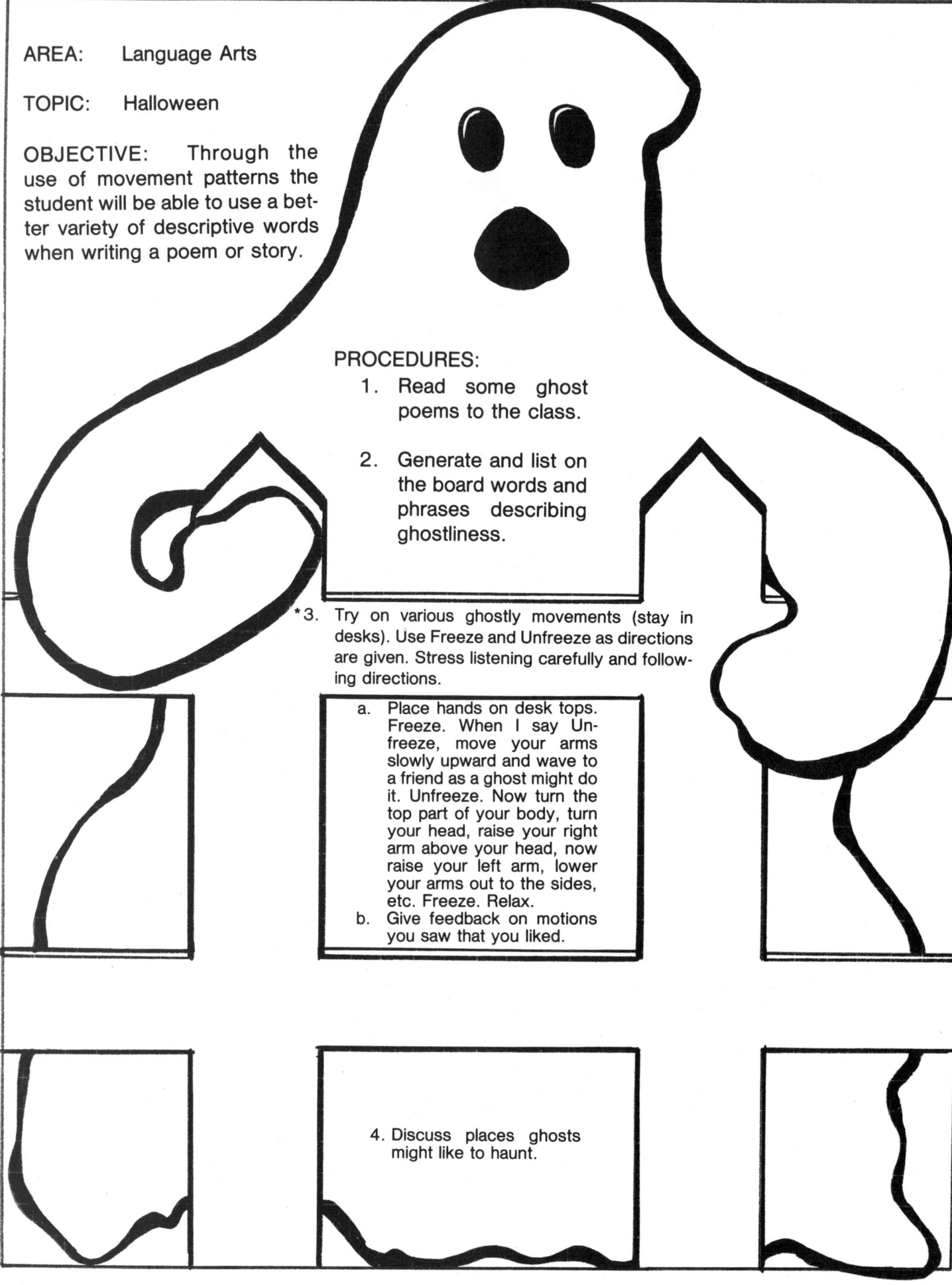

AREA: Language Arts

TOPIC: Halloween

OBJECTIVE: Through the use of movement patterns the student will be able to use a better variety of descriptive words when writing a poem or story.

PROCEDURES:

1. Read some ghost poems to the class.

2. Generate and list on the board words and phrases describing ghostliness.

*3. Try on various ghostly movements (stay in desks). Use Freeze and Unfreeze as directions are given. Stress listening carefully and following directions.

    a. Place hands on desk tops. Freeze. When I say Unfreeze, move your arms slowly upward and wave to a friend as a ghost might do it. Unfreeze. Now turn the top part of your body, turn your head, raise your right arm above your head, now raise your left arm, lower your arms out to the sides, etc. Freeze. Relax.
    b. Give feedback on motions you saw that you liked.

4. Discuss places ghosts might like to haunt.

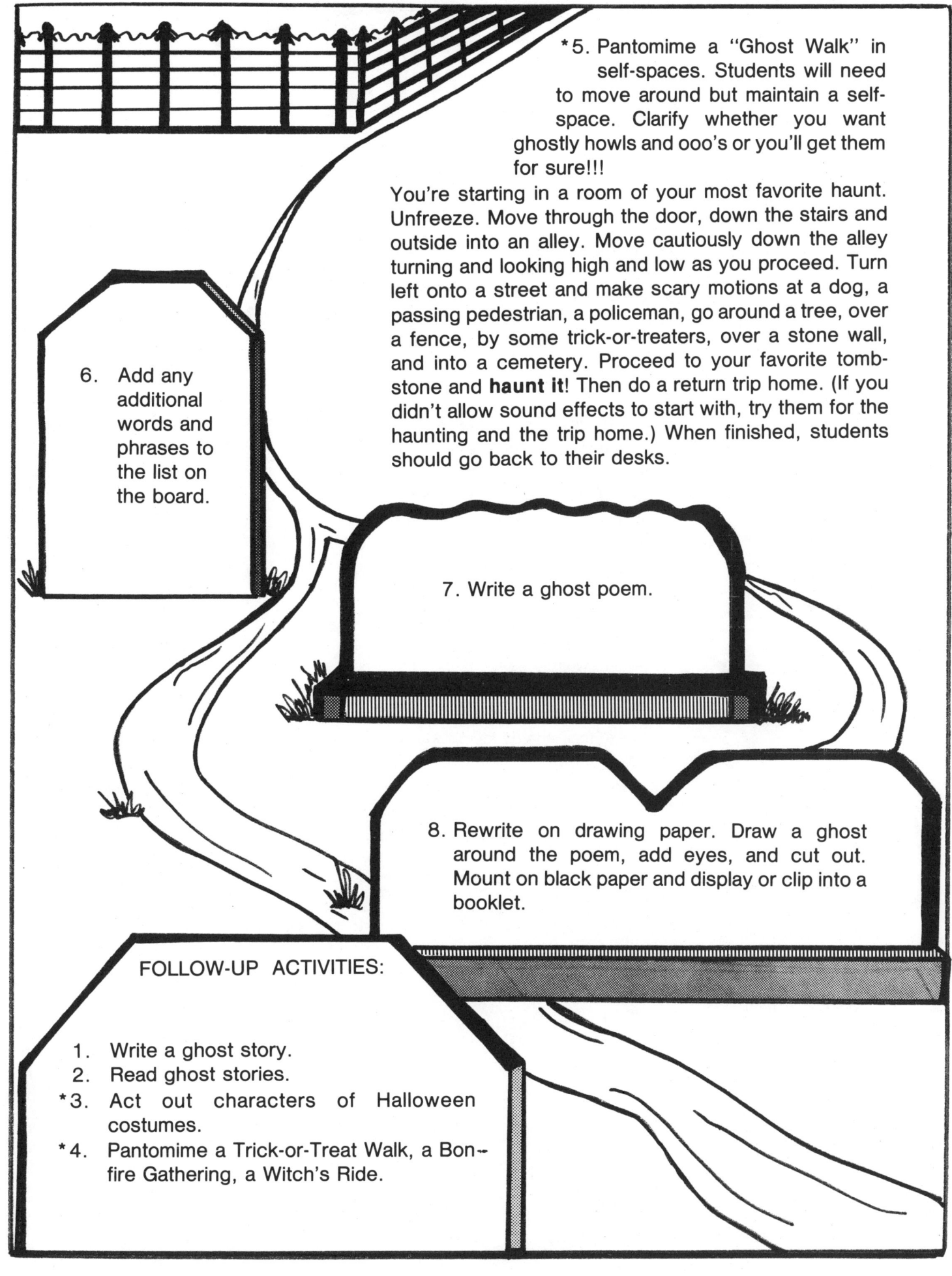

*5. Pantomime a "Ghost Walk" in self-spaces. Students will need to move around but maintain a self-space. Clarify whether you want ghostly howls and ooo's or you'll get them for sure!!!

You're starting in a room of your most favorite haunt. Unfreeze. Move through the door, down the stairs and outside into an alley. Move cautiously down the alley turning and looking high and low as you proceed. Turn left onto a street and make scary motions at a dog, a passing pedestrian, a policeman, go around a tree, over a fence, by some trick-or-treaters, over a stone wall, and into a cemetery. Proceed to your favorite tombstone and **haunt it**! Then do a return trip home. (If you didn't allow sound effects to start with, try them for the haunting and the trip home.) When finished, students should go back to their desks.

6. Add any additional words and phrases to the list on the board.

7. Write a ghost poem.

8. Rewrite on drawing paper. Draw a ghost around the poem, add eyes, and cut out. Mount on black paper and display or clip into a booklet.

FOLLOW-UP ACTIVITIES:

1. Write a ghost story.
2. Read ghost stories.
*3. Act out characters of Halloween costumes.
*4. Pantomime a Trick-or-Treat Walk, a Bonfire Gathering, a Witch's Ride.

Where is my football, my helmet,
my uniform?
Where are my roller skates, my books,
and my other things?
I leave them in one spot but
find them in another.
It must be some invisible being
without a face
That continually moves my things
from place to place.

Tell me, how does a ghost look?
I'm told to view a picture someone took.
Tell me, how does a ghost sound?
I'm told to hear a record that was found.
Tell me, where does a ghost hide?
I'm told to look where no one can reside.
Tell me, how does a ghost travel?
I'm told through things, what a marvel!
Tell me, what does a ghost do all day?
I'm told that they frolic and play.
Tell me, what does a ghost do all night?
I'm told they try to scare you with fright.
Tell me, what does a ghost eat for a meal?
I'm told their energy level doesn't require a great deal.
Tell me, how do I know when a ghost is near?
I'm told funny sensations mean one is near.
Please help me get an answer to each query,
It would help dispel much of which I am wary.

I have a little friend
He follows wherever I go.
To my house he always tends
And lets my happiness show.
He creaks the stairs,
And rattles his chains,
He makes me laugh,
He causes no pain.
He's special cause you see,
Nobody sees him but me!

A very mischievous ghost,
Liked messing things up the most,
Upstairs went downstairs,
Downstairs went upstairs,
And of all his pranks he'd boast.

AREA: Social Studies
TOPIC: Geographical Features
OBJECTIVE: To review/teach concepts of geographical features.

PROCEDURE:

1. Discuss hot air balloons and their ability to ascend above the earth's surface to silently drift with the wind. Usually they float close to the ground providing ample time to observe the ever changing panoramic view from the gondola.

*2. Students pantomime while the teacher narrates the flight. (See following page.) The desks are the gondolas for this ascension.

3. Suggested lessons for instruction:

Let's imagine you see a (steppe, tundra, desert, tropical island, etc.) below. Describe the temperature, rainfall, vegetation, animal life, etc., of this area.

OR

As we ascend, the climate, vegetation, animal life and land features change. Describe sea level. Then describe what happens to the land, vegetation, animal life, temperature, and atmosphere as you rise higher with each blast of the burner.

OR

We're drifting along a coastal area. You see a body of water surrounded on three sides by land. What do you call that body of water? What else do you see (island, port, bay, harbor, small inland lake, etc.)?

The teacher can change from one topic to another (steppe to tundra) by doing the following:

You're still in your gondola and all this time you've been gradually descending as the air cooled inside the envelope. To rise again, pull the blast valve on the burner and the balloon will ascend...(a repeating pattern).

Hot Air Balloon Flight

Your desk is an imaginary gondola of a hot air balloon. You have just completed the required practice flights and course work for your ballooning pilot's license. You've been eagerly awaiting today's solo flight. Can you do it? The weather is perfect! The ground crew has checked out the direction of the drift, unrolled and stretched the envelope out downwind, and checked out the crown deflation port at the top.

Your job is to unpack the instrument panel...install it on the basket rim. Now check to be sure the propane burner is on board and there are no gas leaks.

It's time for inflation. You turn on the ground inflator...the flames thrust hot air into the envelope. Whirrr...the envelope begins to swell and rise. Look up inside; it's a spectacular colorful cavern.

Everything seems in readiness. Imagine you are in the gondola...you turn on the main propane burner that's positioned beneath the skirt by pulling a valve. It spews forth flame and hot air which causes the balloon to swell. It's almost fully inflated now, waiting expectantly for ascension.

As you hold the burner valve open, check the temperature on the pyrometer. It's approaching flight temperature...closer...closer...It's there! The ground crew releases the gondola with a shove and it gradually starts to ascend. Pull the burner blast valve again to rise faster and higher.

Look down at the ground...wave to your crew...Close your eyes...How does it feel? Look down again, it may seem as though the earth is leaving you and not you leaving it. Check the altimeter...the height desired has been attained. Turn down the burner to maintain this height. The roar of the burner lessens and you look around to enjoy, with full appreciation, the almost silent drifting of the balloon.

As you float, you observe the details of the changing panoramic view.
(ADD INSTRUCTIONAL LESSON, SEE #3)

You spot the chase car in the distance below. Point to it.....it's at the designated spot. Cut down on the heat...signal the chase crew you're going to descend...you're approaching, drop the drag line...now you're close to the ground. Pull the ripcord to open the crown deflation port...down goes the gondola onto the ground. You try to keep the gondola upright throughout the landing. The ground crew quickly gathers up the balloon as you climb out. The balloon is packed inside the gondola, loaded onto the truck, and everyone heads for home.

HOT AIR BALLOONS

Gondola -   Straw or metal basket to ride in.

Envelope -   Colorful nylon fabric balloon.

Crown Deflation Port -   Top section of the balloon that opens to allow hot air to quickly
                                   escape for rapid descent.

Ripcord (cord) -   A cord used by the pilot to open the crown deflation port.

Skirt -   Bottom opening portion of the balloon.

Instrument panel -   Altimeter (measures altitude), variometer (rate-of-climb indicator),
                                   pyrometer (measures temperature in the crown of the envelope).

Propane burner -   Heats the air to keep the balloon up; use 2 containers of propane
                                   for approximately 3 hrs. flight.

Inflation -   Add heated air to the balloon.

Deflation -   Release of warm air through the crown port.

Rise -   Caused by heating the air in the envelope.

Descent -   Caused by the cooling of the air in the balloon.

Direction -   Determined by the wind.

Speed -   Determined by the wind.

Adjust Altitude -   Use blasts of heat from the propane burner to raise; lower by allow-
                                   ing air in the balloon to cool.

Stretched out -   Balloon is fully laid out on the ground prior to inflation.

Ascension -   Flight in a hot air balloon.

Attainable Altitude -   Usually stay below 12,000 to 15,000 feet. Need more experience
                                   and oxygen for higher altitudes. Have ascended to heights approx-
                                   imately 32,000 feet.

Wind Speeds -   Low wind speeds are best - less than 10 mph.

AREA: Language Arts/Art
TOPIC: Art

ARF! ARF!

OBJECTIVE: To develop an awareness of and an appreciation for a cartoonist's creativity; the student will create an invention of his own.

PROCEDURE:
1. Have the students generate a list of machine parts.
*2. Try on various machine parts while sitting or standing.
   Example questions:
      How does a piston work?
      What action does a lever have?
      How does a drum move?
   After each question have the children show you that movement using their hands, elbows, arms, legs and heads.

3. Discuss machines that are formed by many synchronized parts working together in unison.
4. Discuss different ways machines start and stop instantaneously or gradually speeding up and slowing down.

*5. Create a class machine:
   a. Decide what this machine is to produce.
   b. Determine who will be at the beginning, position that student and have the student show the class the motion, ask for the next part, put that person in place and have him demonstrate his motion. Try the two together, etc. Encourage variety: high, low, twisting, turning, stamping, sliding, hoisting, swinging.
   c. Determine how the machine starts and stops.
   d. Push the start button, watch the action and "listen to the sounds." It's great!!! Do any necessary side coaching for promoting group togetherness.
   e. Try it to fast and slow music.

*6. Create Group Machines:
   a. Divide students into groups of 5 or 6.
   b. Give them a set time period, a place to work and directions to create a machine. Appoint a person to be in charge.
   c. Have groups demonstrate their machine for the rest of the class.

7. Introduce Rube Goldberg and show the class pictures of his invention-cartoons. Invention-cartoons like these are now known as "Rube Goldbergs."

8. Have students draw an invention-cartoon, adding color. Have them write a sequence of action to match the invention-cartoon.

RESOURCES:
1. Rube Goldberg books.
2. Library books related to unusual machines.
3. Possible films/stories:
   Doughnuts — Homer Price by Robert McCloskey
   The Cat in the Hat by Dr. Seuss
   Dr. Seuss on the Loose (Sneetches) by Dr. Seuss
   Doing It the Hard Way by Rube Goldberg

A. Burglar opens the door.
B. It pulls a string which lets out a glove.
C. The glove punches the dog.
D. The dog runs and pulls the string.
E. The string pulls a bucket.
F. The bucket falls and water pours out.

Byron Beckwith, Age 10

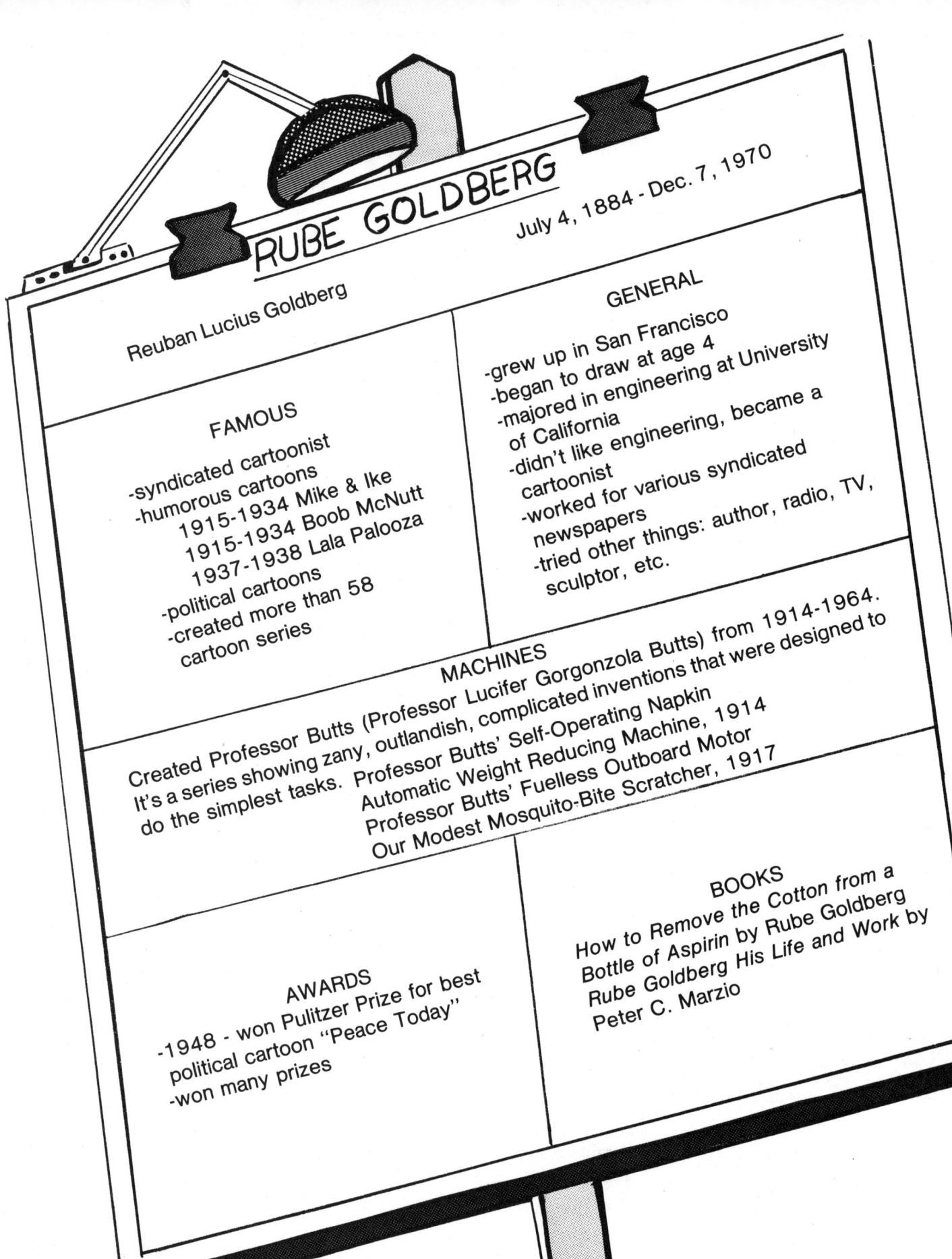

RUBE GOLDBERG

July 4, 1884 - Dec. 7, 1970

Reuban Lucius Goldberg

GENERAL

-grew up in San Francisco
-began to draw at age 4
-majored in engineering at University of California
-didn't like engineering, became a cartoonist
-worked for various syndicated newspapers
-tried other things: author, radio, TV, sculptor, etc.

FAMOUS

-syndicated cartoonist
-humorous cartoons
    1915-1934 Mike & Ike
    1915-1934 Boob McNutt
    1937-1938 Lala Palooza
-political cartoons
-created more than 58 cartoon series

MACHINES

Created Professor Butts (Professor Lucifer Gorgonzola Butts) from 1914-1964. It's a series showing zany, outlandish, complicated inventions that were designed to do the simplest tasks. Professor Butts' Self-Operating Napkin
Automatic Weight Reducing Machine, 1914
Professor Butts' Fuelless Outboard Motor
Our Modest Mosquito-Bite Scratcher, 1917

BOOKS

How to Remove the Cotton from a Bottle of Aspirin by Rube Goldberg
Rube Goldberg His Life and Work by Peter C. Marzio

AWARDS

-1948 - won Pulitzer Prize for best political cartoon "Peace Today"
-won many prizes

AREA: Science

TOPIC: Oceans and Oceanography

OBJECTIVE: To increase the students' knowledge of oceanography and the ocean - its structure and contents.

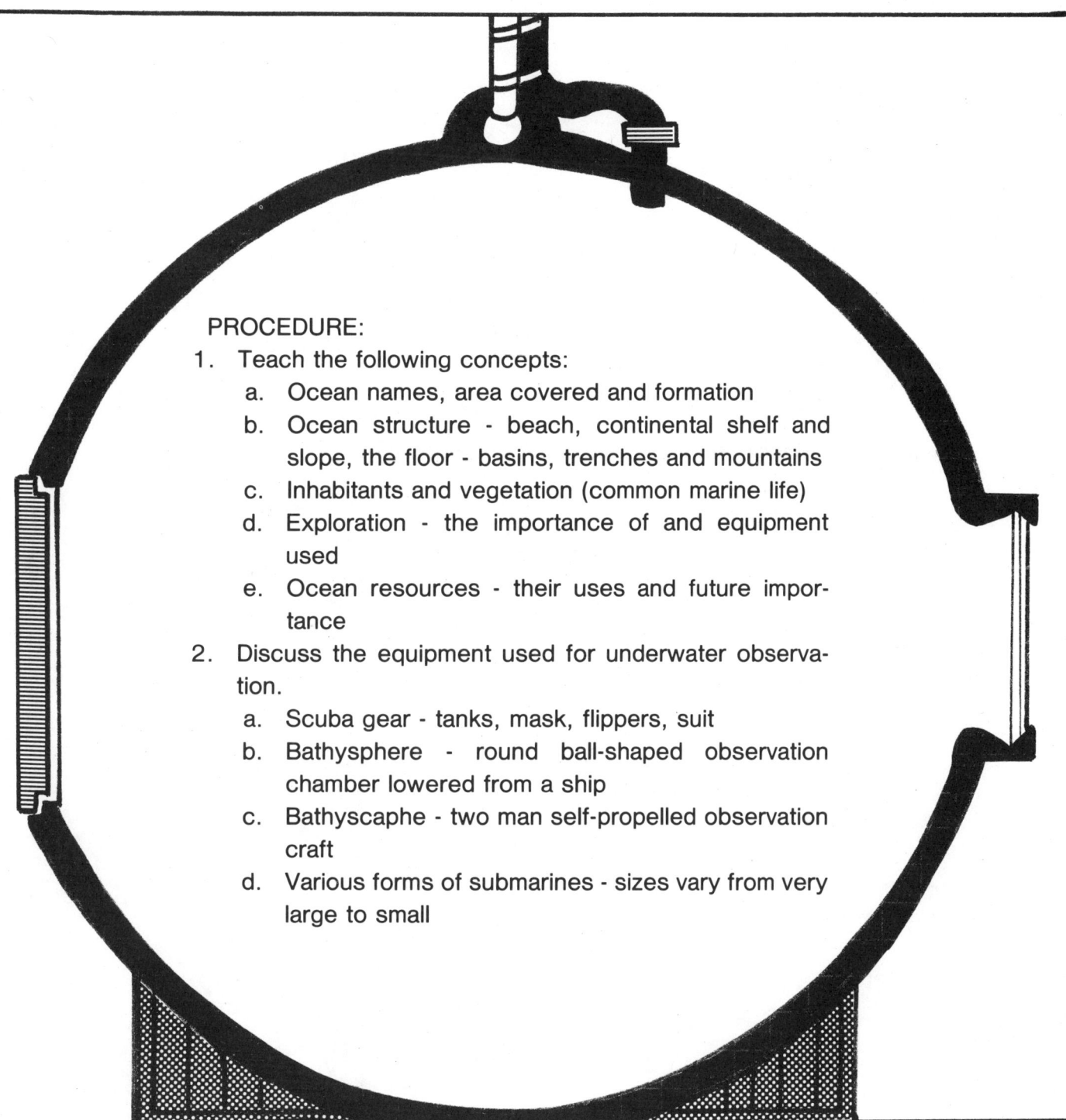

PROCEDURE:

1. Teach the following concepts:
   a. Ocean names, area covered and formation
   b. Ocean structure - beach, continental shelf and slope, the floor - basins, trenches and mountains
   c. Inhabitants and vegetation (common marine life)
   d. Exploration - the importance of and equipment used
   e. Ocean resources - their uses and future importance

2. Discuss the equipment used for underwater observation.
   a. Scuba gear - tanks, mask, flippers, suit
   b. Bathysphere - round ball-shaped observation chamber lowered from a ship
   c. Bathyscaphe - two man self-propelled observation craft
   d. Various forms of submarines - sizes vary from very large to small

3. Introduce three terms used to categorize ocean life and divide the ocean into levels.
   a. Plankton - floaters found near the top
   b. Nekton - swimmers found in the upper and middle levels
   c. Benthos - crawlers found on or near the ocean floor

4. List the three categories on the board and have students generate a list of common marine plants and animals found in each.

*5. The students pantomime while the teacher narrates a deep-sea observation trip in a bathysphere. (See following page.)

6. Students complete Observation Report following their pantomimed trip. (See Activity Page.)

FOLLOW-UP ACTIVITIES:
1. Try this narration-type lesson using a different type of observation equipment such as a mini or large sub.
2. Use a different focus for observation, such as the ocean floor - the continental shelf, slope, basin, trenches and mountains.
3. Become a deep sea or sponge diver. Write about an unusual experience.
4. Illustrate different types of equipment used in oceanography.
5. Make a list of important minerals, food, and products we receive from the ocean.
6. Make a prediction about the future importance of the ocean.
7. Make a poster to show the food chain or pyramid of life in the ocean.

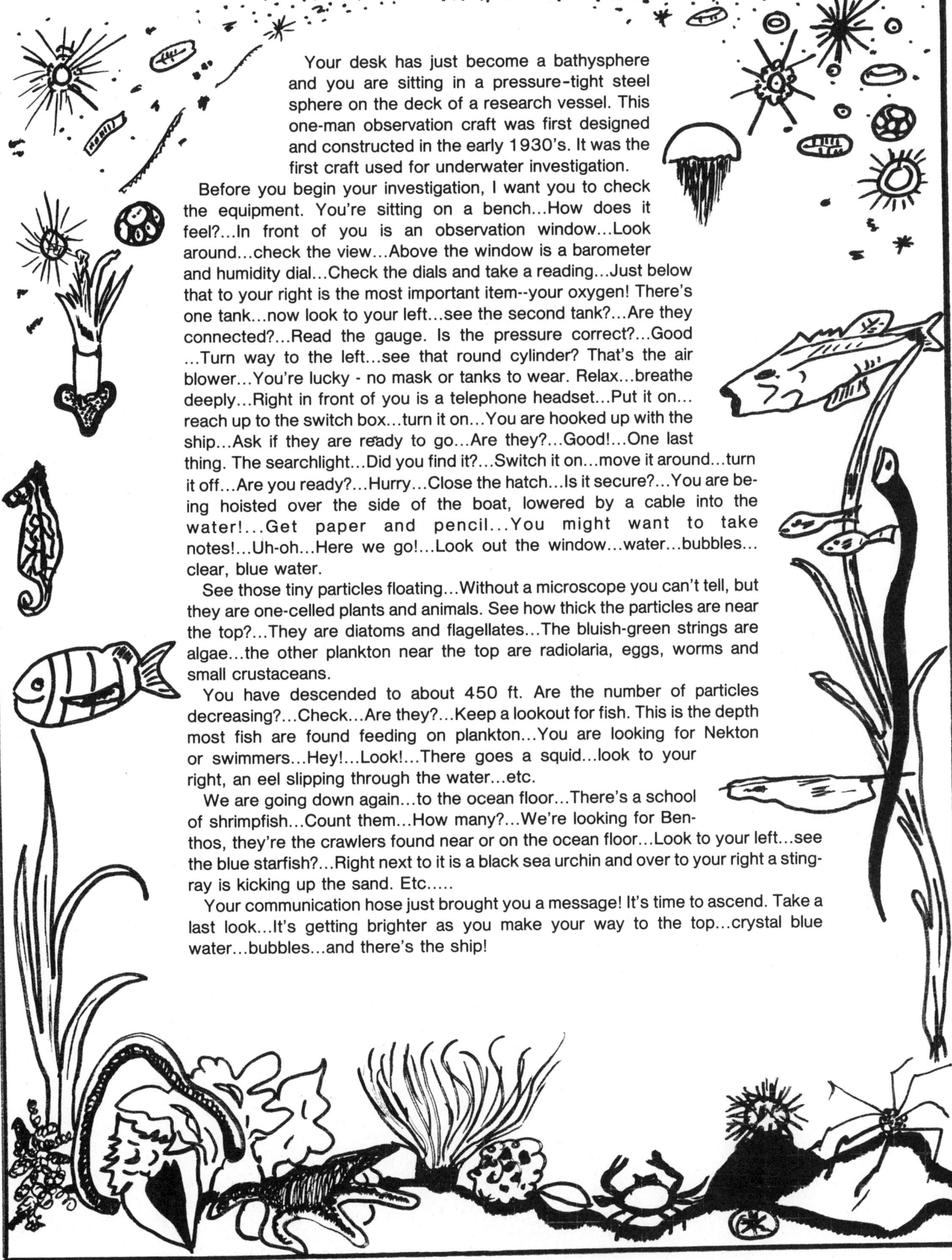

Your desk has just become a bathysphere and you are sitting in a pressure-tight steel sphere on the deck of a research vessel. This one-man observation craft was first designed and constructed in the early 1930's. It was the first craft used for underwater investigation.

Before you begin your investigation, I want you to check the equipment. You're sitting on a bench...How does it feel?...In front of you is an observation window...Look around...check the view...Above the window is a barometer and humidity dial...Check the dials and take a reading...Just below that to your right is the most important item--your oxygen! There's one tank...now look to your left...see the second tank?...Are they connected?...Read the gauge. Is the pressure correct?...Good ...Turn way to the left...see that round cylinder? That's the air blower...You're lucky - no mask or tanks to wear. Relax...breathe deeply...Right in front of you is a telephone headset...Put it on... reach up to the switch box...turn it on...You are hooked up with the ship...Ask if they are ready to go...Are they?...Good!...One last thing. The searchlight...Did you find it?...Switch it on...move it around...turn it off...Are you ready?...Hurry...Close the hatch...Is it secure?...You are being hoisted over the side of the boat, lowered by a cable into the water!...Get paper and pencil...You might want to take notes!...Uh-oh...Here we go!...Look out the window...water...bubbles... clear, blue water.

See those tiny particles floating...Without a microscope you can't tell, but they are one-celled plants and animals. See how thick the particles are near the top?...They are diatoms and flagellates...The bluish-green strings are algae...the other plankton near the top are radiolaria, eggs, worms and small crustaceans.

You have descended to about 450 ft. Are the number of particles decreasing?...Check...Are they?...Keep a lookout for fish. This is the depth most fish are found feeding on plankton...You are looking for Nekton or swimmers...Hey!...Look!...There goes a squid...look to your right, an eel slipping through the water...etc.

We are going down again...to the ocean floor...There's a school of shrimpfish...Count them...How many?...We're looking for Ben-thos, they're the crawlers found near or on the ocean floor...Look to your left...see the blue starfish?...Right next to it is a black sea urchin and over to your right a sting-ray is kicking up the sand. Etc.....

Your communication hose just brought you a message! It's time to ascend. Take a last look...It's getting brighter as you make your way to the top...crystal blue water...bubbles...and there's the ship!

OBSERVATION REPORT

TOPIC: SEA LIFE

NAME:

DATE: TIME:

BODY OF WATER:

TYPE OF EQUIPMENT USED:

Write the definition of each term and illustrate at least five specimens you observed in each category.

PLANKTON -

NEKTON -

BENTHOS -

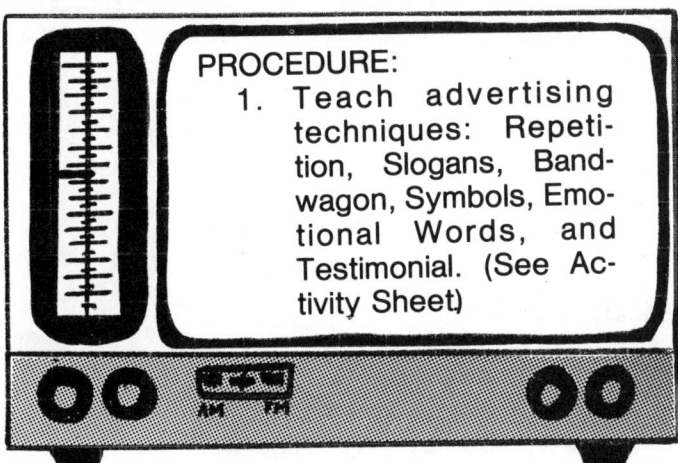

PROCEDURE:
1. Teach advertising techniques: Repetition, Slogans, Bandwagon, Symbols, Emotional Words, and Testimonial. (See Activity Sheet)

THE STATE JOURNAL SCENE LANSING, MICH.

ENTERTAINMENT GUIDE

2. Students create advertisements. Have students:
   a. Select a product.
   b. Create a brand name.
   c. Create a magazine advertisement for their product. Put it on drawing paper. Should be able to identify the technique used in their ad.
   d. Write a TV/radio commercial for their product. Should be able to identify advertising technique used.

*3. Groups act out the commercials.
   a. Divide into groups; the ad writer chooses needed helpers.
   b. The groups plan, prepare props, and practice.
   c. Act out the commercial for the class. Stress the need to stay in character throughout the entire commercial.
   d. The class guesses the advertising technique used in the commercial. Discuss its use.
   e. Evaluate with the class.

FOLLOW-UP ACTIVITIES:
1. Create an advertisement promoting your class as the best in the school. Use various advertising techniques to do this. Consider the decor and the clientele: the arrangement, the furnishings, the mental and physical abilities of the students, the teacher.
2. Be radio announcers and do created radio commercials.

Directions: Make up your own advertisements.

Symbol:	Repetition:
Testimonial:	Bandwagon:
Slogan:	Emotional Words:

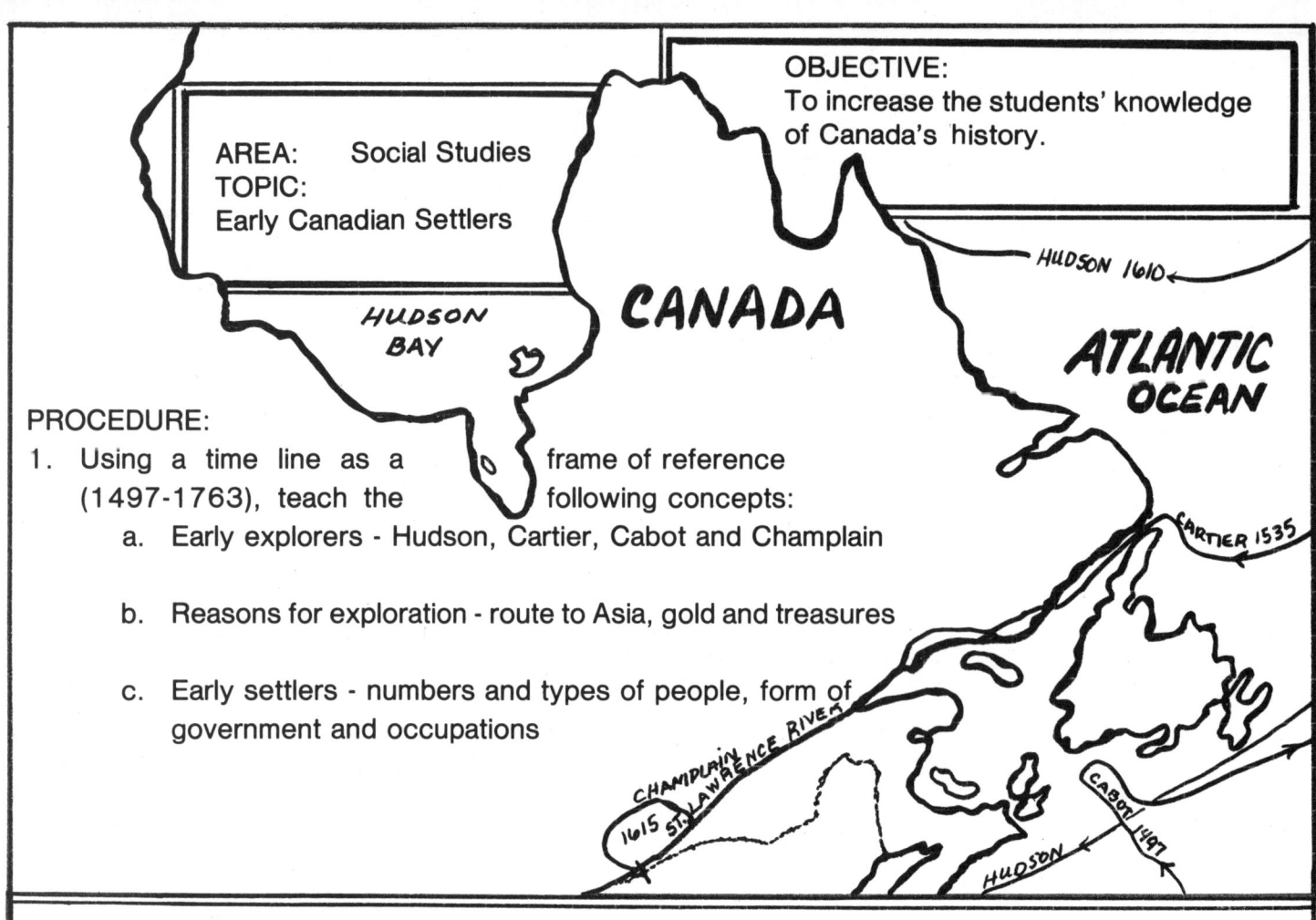

AREA: Social Studies
TOPIC:
Early Canadian Settlers

OBJECTIVE:
To increase the students' knowledge
of Canada's history.

HUDSON 1610

CANADA

ATLANTIC
OCEAN

HUDSON
BAY

CARTIER 1535

PROCEDURE:

1. Using a time line as a frame of reference (1497-1763), teach the following concepts:

   a. Early explorers - Hudson, Cartier, Cabot and Champlain

   b. Reasons for exploration - route to Asia, gold and treasures

   c. Early settlers - numbers and types of people, form of government and occupations

CHAMPLAIN ST. LAWRENCE RIVER 1615

CABOT 1497

HUDSON

2. Discuss the various occupations of the French and English settlers - for example, farmers, fishermen, trappers, housewives, missionaries, traders, etc. Include the hours, skills, tools and personal qualities required.

*3. Try on characters. Have all the students find a self-space and pantomime the character described. Use side coaching to help develop the appropriate movements, expressions and details of the character they are portraying. After going through all the characters, pick out students to share their characterizations in front of the class. Examples:

   a. A cold, sore, tired English fisherman unhappy about the day's catch.

   b. A French trapper carrying furs to the trading post.

   c. A tired farmer putting away tools at the end of a long day.

   d. A busy, hard-working English mother doing chores around the house.

* 4. Role play occupational situations.
    a. Describe a working situation involving 2-4 people.
    b. Discuss the situation and suggestions for acting it out.
    c. Pick the students and assign the roles and the area to be used.
    d. Give the students 2 or 3 minutes to talk over their plan of action. The improvisations may need your guidance, especially the first one.
    e. When the students are set, give them the cue "Curtain Up" to start the action.
    f. When they finish, discuss what they liked, disliked, and any possible changes. Repeat the same situation, if you like, with new students and changes or go on to a new situation.

    Possible Situations:

    It's a cold, windy, early spring morning. Three English fishermen are walking from their homes to the dock where their boat is kept. They are carrying some equipment and their lunch. They arrive at the boat, load their supplies and cast off. After spending a short time fishing without success, a storm comes up so they have to return home.

    On a cold winter day, three French trappers get bundled up, gather their equipment and set out walking through heavy snow to check their traps. They pick up several beavers, reset the traps and head back to camp. They skin the animals and place them on drying racks. They make a trip to the trading post for supplies and to sell a few furs.

5. Have the students list 6 occupations of the early settlers and their qualifications. (See Activity Page.)

FARMER   HOUSEWIFE   BLACKSMITH   MISSIONARY   MINISTER

TRADER   SOLDIER   GOVERNMENTAL OFFICIAL   EXPLORER

TRAPPER   CARPENTER   PRIEST   PARENT

FOLLOW-UP ACTIVITIES:
1. Write a factual description of one occupation.
2. Pretend you are a trapper. Write five journal entries describing your job.
3. Make an advertisement for a job opening. Describe the job, location, hours, pay and other benefits.

After listing 6 occupations of the French/English settlers, complete the chart.

OCCUPATION	HOURS	SKILLS/TOOLS	PERSONAL QUALITIES REQUIRED

114

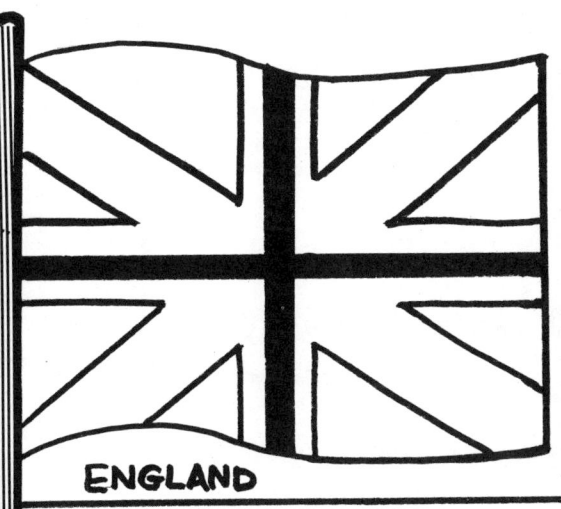

ENGLAND

AREA: Social Studies

TOPIC: Canada - French/English Rivalry
French and Indian War

OBJECTIVE: To increase the students' knowledge of the French and Indian War

PROCEDURE:

1. Review early settlements of the French and English. Discuss their similarities and differences. (See Fact Sheet)

2. Discuss the rivalry (disagreements and quarrels) over
   a. Coastal fishing rights
   b. Use of drying spots
   c. Trapping rights
   d. Land use and ownership.

*3. Try on characters. As a whole class have the students practice being -
   A. A French/English fisherman loading a boat, casting off, fishing, pulling in fish, unloading the catch, cleaning and drying the fish.
   b. A French/English trapper carrying equipment, setting traps, removing an animal, placing a skin on a drying rack, traveling through the woods, loading furs to take to the trading post.
   c. An angry person, showing the movements, gestures, and facial expressions during an imaginary quarrel. A helpful pantomimed example: on television, a baseball player arguing with an umpire.

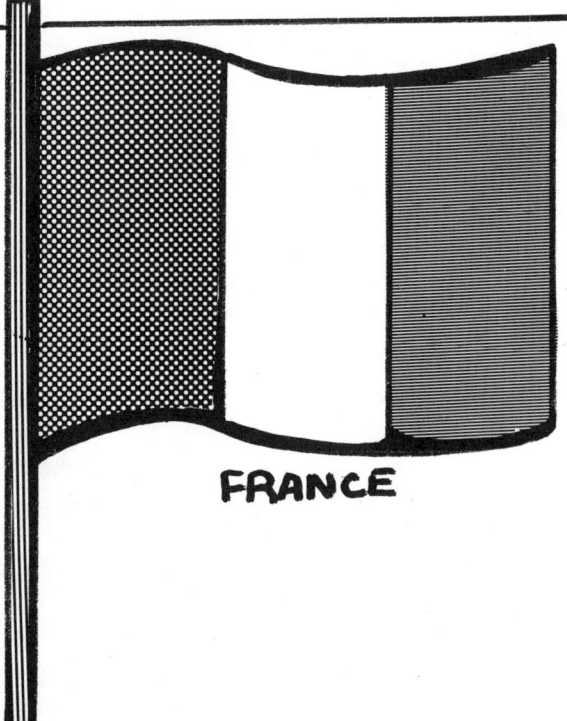

FRANCE

*4. Role play small group situations. One group is English, the other French and they are disagreeing and quarreling.

GOOD RULE - No physical contact.

Examples:

    a. A boat of Englishmen fishing and a boat of Frenchmen come and claim it's their territory.

    b. On the beach a disagreement about ownership of a drying spot. Frenchmen are cleaning and drying their fish and a group of Englishmen claim it's their spot.

    c. Several French trappers find extra traps in their area. They then run into English trappers and quarrel about whose area it is.

5. Complete the Activity Sheet.

6. You have set the background for the French and Indian War and could easily act out the last and most important battle - "The Battle of Quebec."

    a. Discuss advantages/disadvantages of each side.

    b. Discuss the location of the battle, leaders and participants. (French, English and Indians)

    c. Try on characters.

    d. Set the scenes - the area in the room where the fort and the battlefield are.

    e. Assign roles and pantomime the battle.

The students enjoy doing this and it helps them understand and retain it.

FOLLOW-UP ACTIVITIES:

    1. Make a time line of Canada's history.

    2. Pretend they're historians telling the reasons for the French and Indian War.

    3. Write an account of the Battle of Quebec from an Indian, French or Englishman's point of view.

FACT SHEET: SIMILARITIES AND DIFFERENCES BETWEEN THE FRENCH AND ENGLISH COLONIES

COLONIES	SIMILARITIES	DIFFERENCES
ENGLISH	Climate and Location Reasons for settling - Better life Fortunes Type of people - Adventurous Hardworking Types of occupations - Farmers Fishermen Trappers	Welcomed all types of people Owned their own land Established self-rule Few governmental rules and regulations Enjoyed many freedoms Church of England
FRENCH	Established forts and trading posts Sent exports to Europe Faced dangers - Wilderness Hostile Indians Recreation - Games, Songs, Stories and Contests	No undesirables allowed Large estates limited large ownership No voice in colonial government Strict governmental rules and regulations Limited freedoms Sparsely populated Sent missionaries - Roman Catholic

LIST THE REASONS FOR THE FRENCH/INDIAN WAR.

CHOOSE A SIDE:

Write a paragraph telling if you think you will win or lose. Give your reasons why.

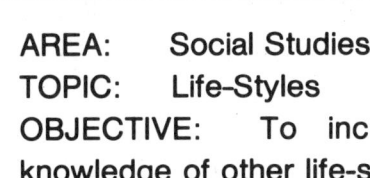

AREA: Social Studies
TOPIC: Life-Styles
OBJECTIVE: To increase the students' awareness and knowledge of other life-styles and cultures (Eskimo)
NOTE: This lesson can be adapted to other cultures.

PROCEDURE:

1. Teach the following concepts about a culture (Eskimo):
   a. Location and climate - the average temperatures, land forms, vegetation and animal life of the region
   b. Main diet - coastal inhabitants - seals and whales, inland inhabitants - caribou
   c. Housing - their temporary shelters and permanent homes
   d. Clothing - names and descriptions of articles worn
   e. Occupations - importance of hunting, tools and skills required
   f. Forms of transportation - the dog sled vs. the snowmobile
   g. Family life - customs, education, recreation, daily routine

2. Discuss "A Day in the Life of an Eskimo Child." Review the daily routine starting as the child gets up in the morning until he goes to bed at night. Compare it to the students' own daily schedules. Discuss similarities and differences.
   NOTE: Especially for the Eskimo culture be sure to have modern, up-to-date information.

3. Review with the class what a play or skit is. Discuss how it can be separated into scenes and can be pantomimed, contain dialogue or be narrated.

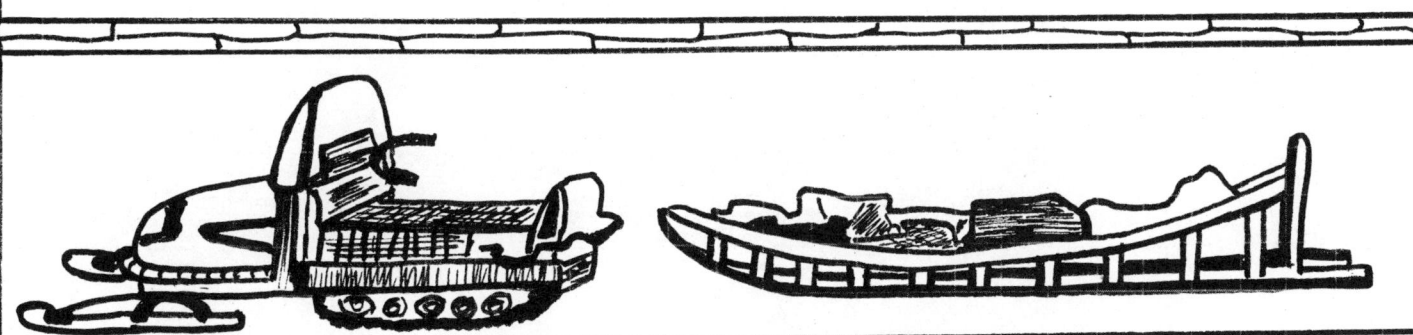

4. Explain to the class that in a small group they are going to write a skit and perform it for the class. The topic is "A Day in the Life of an Eskimo Family." It must include or show the following information:
   a. Names of characters
   b. A location and setting
   c. Occupation of the family
   d. Form of transportation
   e. Diet and type of home
   f. Family life - education, customs, recreation

   The skit must be separated into 5 scenes - such as breakfast time, a hunting party, making and mending clothes, children at school, or an evening of storytelling.

*5. Divide the class into groups of 4 or 5 students. As a group they write the scenes, assign the character roles, and decide if it will be pantomimed, contain dialogue or be narrated. NOTE: This takes several class periods and the teacher acts as a source of information.

*6. After the skit is written and checked for information a good complete copy must be turned in. The groups are given time to practice before presenting to the class. Practice can take place in the hall or a free space in the room. An area in the room is designated as the stage, and during the days of practice each group must rotate to the stage and work with the teacher. At this point side coaching and setting the scenes are done. This takes about a week (40-minute time periods).

*7. Final Performance: This is a culminating activity to a unit and is a good evaluation of the students' knowledge of a culture. The skits can be presented to just your class or you may wish to invite parents or students from other classrooms. You'll find the students excited and you'll be impressed.

BIBLIOGRAPHY

Dixon, Peter L. with Jay Fiondella, *Ballooning*, New York: Ballantine Books, 1972.

Dugan, James, *World Beneath the Sea,* Washington, D.C.: National Geographic Society, 1973.

Gaskell, T. F., *World Beneath the Ocean*, Garden City, N.Y.: The National History Press, 1964.

Joyce, William and W. Robert Houston, Herbert H. Gross, Susan Dye Lee, *Exploring Regions of Latin America and Canada*, Chicago: Follett Educational Corporation, 1971.

McGovern, Ann, *...if you sailed on the Mayflower*, New York: Four Winds Press, 1969.

Radlauer, Ed and Ruth, *Hot Air Balloons,* Glendale, California: Bowmar, 1974.

Rothe, Anna, Editor, *Current Biography Who's News and Why*, New York: The H. W. Wilson Co., 1948 and 1970.